The Anti-Bullying and Teasing Book for Preschool Classrooms

Acknowledgments

We would like to thank the following people from the Howley School-Preschool and Child Care Center in Trenton, New Jersey, who helped to pilot-test the activities for this book: Lisa Cipriano-Rogalski, Assistant Director, and teachers Sharon Dunlap, Valerie Maher, Patricia Mallozzi, Diane Rothschild, and Jean Scott.

In addition, we would like to express our appreciation to Dr. Herman Hinitz for taking the photographs at the Howley School.

The Anti-Bullying and Teasing Book for Preschool Classrooms

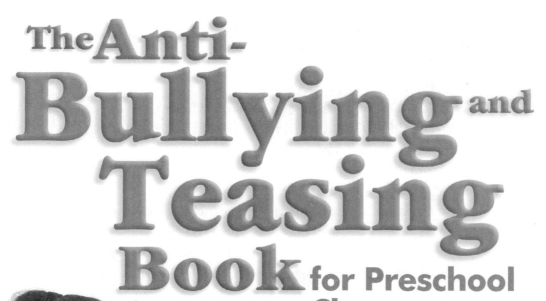

Barbara Sprung and Merle Froschl with Dr. Blythe Hinitz

Illustrations: Kathy Dobbs

Photographs: Mary Duru and Dr. Herman Hinitz

gryphon house, inc.

Beltsville, Maryland

© 2005 Barbara Sprung and Merle Froschl, with Dr. Blythe Hinitz
Printed in the United States of America.

Published by Gryphon House, Inc.
10726 Tucker Street, Beltsville, MD 20705
301.595.9500; 301.595.0051 (fax); 800.638.0928 (toll-free)

Visit us on the web at www.gryphonhouse.com

Library of Congress Cataloging in Publication Data

Sprung, Barbara.

The anti-bullying and teasing book for preschool classrooms / by Barbara Sprung, Merle Froschl, with Blythe Hinitz ; photographs by Mary Duru ; illustrations by Kathy Dobbs.

p. cm.

Summary: "Resource book for preschool teachers that provides activities and techniques to prevent and address teasing and bullying in the classroom"--Provided by publisher. Includes bibliographical references and index.

ISBN 0-87659-242-6

1. Bullying in school--Prevention. 2. Teasing--Prevention. 3. Education, Preschool--Activity programs. I. Froschl, Merle. II. Hinitz, Blythe Simone Farb, 1944- III. Title.

LB3013.3.S67 2005

371.5'8--dc22

2005002659

Table of Contents

Introduction

Stop It Before It Starts

In preschool, children encounter their first experiences in forming and joining social groups outside their family. What a wonderful opportunity you have as a teacher to help them do it right!

As a teacher, you have a major influence on how children view themselves within the larger world. Children take their cues from you, reflecting your language and interactions with them and with other adults. By creating a climate of mutual respect, you can help children learn to develop empathy and treat others fairly and kindly. You can help them learn not to tease and bully each other, and to stand up for themselves and their friends in safe and developmentally appropriate ways.

The Anti-Bullying and Teasing Book will help you create a school environment in which all children feel comfortable, safe, and welcome. In her article entitled, "True Blue," M. Christine Mattise (2004) points out how important it is to a child's sense of safety and well-being to create an environment that sends the following messages:

- If you are hurt on the playground, someone will come to see if you are all right.
- If you are alone, you are welcome to join in a game.
- If you are being teased, other children will come and tell the teaser to stop.
- If you need help, ask an adult.

Creating a caring environment at the beginning of the school year reduces the need for children to assert themselves through negative behavior such as teasing and bullying. As an educator of young children, you can address this behavior before it takes root and grows.

Consequences

The 1999 shootings at Columbine High School—along with other horrific acts of school violence—have provided a wake-up call for the entire country. The fact that all the perpetrators of this violence had been teased and bullied—called names, excluded, picked on—focused national attention on the damaging consequences of what had been considered by many to be a normal part of growing up. Teasing and bullying, however, are not harmless behaviors. They can affect a child's learning, physical health, and emotional well-being. In a classroom, teasing and bullying create a climate that makes it hard to teach and even harder to learn.

School should always be a friendly, welcoming place for a child, but it is not for a child who is teased and bullied there. If a child is worried about what's going to happen at school, he or she will have trouble concentrating, begin to dislike school, and may want to avoid going altogether. Children who are teased and bullied can develop physical symptoms, such as headaches and stomachaches. Emotionally, a child can become sad, withdrawn, anxious, and depressed. Teasing and bullying can create lasting scars for victims, affecting their personal and professional lives as adults.

As Terence P. Thornberry states in the 1994 *Carnegie Quarterly* "Saving Youth from Violence" issue, "Violence does not drop out of the sky. It is part of a long developmental process that begins in early childhood." In a recent article in *Childhood Education,* James Bullock writes, "Considering that bullying often is a sign that aggressive or violent behavior is present elsewhere in children's lives—young children may be acting out at school what they have observed and learned in the home—and the fact that bullying among primary school-age children is now recognized as an antecedent to progressively more violent behavior in later grades, it behooves teachers to take notice." It also makes it imperative to include family members in the efforts to address teasing and bullying behavior in preschool.

Defining Teasing and Bullying

Teasing and bullying are acts that occur over time, or a single unprovoked act in which physical, verbal, or exclusionary behavior is used by one or more children to intimidate, make fun of or intervene with what another child or children are doing. In this guide, teasing and bullying are addressed as a continuum of intentionally hurtful behavior. At one end of the continuum, teasing can take the form of making fun of someone. At the other end, bullying can take the form of repetitive physical abuse. Along the continuum, teasing can include calling someone names, using put-downs, or ridiculing another person. Further along this continuum is verbal bullying, which could include making threats or insulting family members. Bullying can also be psychological—intentionally excluding someone or telling lies about them. And, of course, physical—making faces, gesturing, hitting, pushing, or shoving.

Some people believe that there is a form of teasing that can be playful, even "helpful," in terms of preparing children to cope later on. However, we feel this distinction does not hold with children as young as three and four, and that a better approach in preschool is to create a teasing-free environment. *The Anti-Bullying and Teasing Book* is inspired by the work of Vivian Gussin Paley, a highly-experienced early childhood educator who has written many books about how young children learn social behavior. In her Kindergarten classroom, Paley created a bottom-line rule that no child may exclude another for any reason. She took the bold step of telling children, "You can't say you can't play," which then became the title of her well-known book. As a result, in the course of one school year, children in her class became inclusive rather than exclusive in their play and were free to take on less rigid gender roles.

Teasing and bullying are prevalent in classrooms worldwide, and much of the research has been conducted outside the United States and with older children. However, a recent study conducted by Educational Equity Concepts and Wellesley Centers for Research on Women investigated teasing and bullying behavior in children grades K-3 in classrooms in New York and Massachusetts. Methodology included classroom observations, children's interviews, and focus groups with teachers and parents (Gropper and Froschl, 2000). Findings of this study, which parallel those of other studies that have been conducted both within and outside the United States, include:

- Teasing and bullying are frequent occurrences in grades K-3 (4.6 incidents were observed every three hours).

Teasing includes making fun of someone, calling someone names, using put-downs, or ridiculing another person.

Bullying can take the form of repetitive physical, verbal, or psychological abuse—gesturing, hitting, pushing, shoving, insulting, or excluding.

- Boys initiate most of the teasing and bullying incidents (three times as often as girls).
- Girls and boys are equally likely to be recipients.
- Boys are more likely to respond physically, while girls are more likely to respond verbally to incidents initiated against them.
- Although adults are present, there is a consistent lack of adult intervention in the observed incidents (adults were uninvolved 71% of the time).
- Children feel that adults do not pay attention or support them in ways that resolve the teasing and bullying.
- Children want adults to become more involved.

Being a Bystander

Being in the role of a bystander—someone who watches or participates on the sidelines by laughing or taunting as a child is being teased or bullied—also has a negative effect on children. Often, adults get so caught up in the incident, talking to the aggressor and comforting the hurt child, that the role of the bystanders is overlooked. Children who stand by while a friend is being teased and bullied may be uneasy or even scared that they might be next. They feel powerless if they do nothing to help. They learn negative ways to interact with others—they attach themselves to the teaser who seems to have power or who may be seen as a popular person. As their teacher, you have the opportunity to work with bystanders, helping them to develop the inner strength to do the right thing and stand up for a friend. As a result, children will become more able to stand up for themselves and not tolerate teasing and bullying behavior.

Gender Plays a Role

The results of the previous study, as well as other research with older students, point out the need for sensitivity to issues of gender when addressing teasing and bullying behavior in your classroom. While both girls and boys engage in teasing and bullying behavior, research suggests that boys are more frequently involved in physical or "direct" bullying and girls experience more exclusionary or "indirect" behavior.

The fact is that while both girls and boys are the targets, boys initiate most of the teasing and bullying. Children are aware of what is going on—they know who is teasing and bullying whom. In the words of one kindergartner: "Boys chase girls, because that's what boys do, they chase." Children are also aware that adults are not paying adequate attention. "Teachers don't do anything," explained one kindergartner. "Kids won't stop until the teacher makes them."

Given this situation, it is most likely that children come away with the message that teasing and bullying are condoned. It is also likely that children internalize that teachers are giving boys license to behave in these ways.

Families Matter

Parents are their children's first teachers. This statement is probably most true when it relates to children's behavior toward one another. Before they enter your classroom, children will have learned valuable life lessons already: what is safe, what is dangerous, what is right, what is wrong. Home-school communication is never as great as it is in preschool. This gives you the chance to engage parents in the development of a caring community and to reinforce teachings about empathy and mutual respect.

You can create a partnership between home and school and build a foundation for talking about important issues that affect all children's lives.

You Can Make a Difference

A basic role of education is to help children learn to live together peacefully, solve problems cooperatively, and prepare to be productive citizens of the world. According to the National Association for the Education of Young Children (NAEYC) Code of Ethical Conduct, these goals can be stated in terms of "democratic life skills," which include the ability to:

- see one's self as a worthy individual and a capable member of the group
- express strong emotions in non-hurting ways
- solve problems ethically and intelligently
- be understanding of the feeling and viewpoints of others
- work cooperatively in groups, with acceptance of the human differences among members.

All children deserve a school that is a caring and welcoming place. By creating a classroom environment that fosters respect, kindness, and cooperation, and by engaging in a proactive curriculum to prevent teasing and bullying, you can make it so.

References

Bullock, J. R. Spring 2002. Bullying among children. ***Childhood Education,*** 73(3).

Ching, C. April 2002. ***A qualitative study on bullying.*** A thesis submitted to the Department of Education, Chaminade University.

Cipriano-Rogalski, L. Spring 2004. ***"Stop it or . . . I'm telling!"*** ECED 640 [Advanced Child Development] research paper. The College of New Jersey.

Freedman, J. S. 2002. ***Easing the teasing.*** New York: Contemporary Books.

Froschl, M. & B. Sprung. 1999. On purpose: Addressing teasing and bullying in early childhood. ***Young Children*** 54(2): 70-72.

Froschl, M., B. Sprung, & N. Mullin-Rindler. 1998. ***Quit it! A teacher's guide on teasing and bullying for use with students in grades K-3.*** (A joint publication of Educational Equity Concepts, Inc., Wellesley College Center for Research on Women, NEA Professional Library) New York: Educational Equity Concepts, Inc.

Gartrell, D. 2001. Replacing time-out: Part one—using guidance to build an encouraging classroom. ***Young Children*** 56(6): 8-17.

Gropper, N., & M. Froschl. April 2000. Teasing and bullying behavior in early education. ***Equity and Excellence in Education.***

Hinitz, B. & C. Ching Hangai. August 2004. ***Developing and using anti-bullying/anti-harassment strategies with pre-service and in-service teachers.*** Juried paper presented at the World Organization for Early Childhood Education (OMEP) XXIV World Congress, Melbourne, Australia.

Katch, J. 2003. ***They don't like me.*** Boston, MA: Beacon Press.

Mattise, M. C. Spring 2004. True blue: An American educator brings her anti-bullying program to South African schools. ***Teaching Tolerance,*** issue 25.

Paley, V. 1992. ***You can't say you can't play.*** Cambridge, MA: Harvard University Press.

Thornberry, T. P. Winter 1994. Saving youth from violence. ***Carnegie Quarterly,*** vol. XXXIX, No. 1.

CHAPTER I

How to Use This Guide

The Anti-Bullying and Teasing Book is a guide to help you make your preschool classroom a caring and safe environment where all children feel welcome, accepted, and respected. Young children do not come into a preschool setting knowing how to express their thoughts and feelings verbally, how to sit and listen to a story and participate in a discussion about it. It takes time for them to develop these skills, but it is well worth the time and effort.

Teachable Moments

The Anti-Bullying and Teasing Book presents opportunities to explain, clarify, and expand children's knowledge base. Think of these opportunities as "teachable moments." Teachable moments are the times when you stop a lesson to explain the meaning of a word that is new to the children, enlarging and enriching their vocabularies. They are times when a child asks you an interesting question and you bring it up at a circle or meeting time for discussion. Or, when you notice an act of kindness on the playground and use that to encourage pro-social behavior among all of the children. Teachable moments are precious tools that can and should be used spontaneously to enhance the daily curriculum for you and the children.

Classroom Environment

Chapter 2 discusses the important role that circle or meeting time plays in building a classroom community. It contains suggestions for rethinking learning centers—Blocks, Dramatic Play, and the Outdoors—to increase creative play and cooperation. The chapter also contains instructions for setting up two areas—a "Let's Work It Out Table" and a "Let's Calm Down Corner"—that can help to create a caring, safe, and welcoming environment in your classroom.

"Let's Work It Out" Table

This is a table and two or three chairs, set in a quiet area of the classroom where children can learn beginning negotiating skills and verbal strategies for resolving conflicts peacefully, first with adult help and then, as they gain experience, on their own. Children learn the rules for using the table and can use stick puppets to help them role-play different situations. Just the fact that there is a "Let's Work It Out" table right in the classroom gives a strong message to children that words are the acceptable tools for resolving conflicts.

"Let's Calm Down" Corner

The "Let's Calm Down" corner is a quiet place in the classroom where children can go to reduce feelings of tension or anger by listening to music, hugging a stuffed animal, looking at picture books, or working with clay. For some children, being in the stimulating environment of a preschool classroom for several hours a day can be too much of a good thing, and they may need some time alone. For other children, there may be something upsetting happening at home or they may have had a conflict in the play yard that made them feel angry or tense. The "Let's Calm Down" corner can be a place for these children to go until they feel centered and ready to rejoin the group. At first, you might have to suggest that someone go to that area, but eventually children should be able to choose to go to the area independently.

Family Involvement

A family letter to introduce this program is in Chapter 3, Family Involvement. In addition, letters for each theme in the curriculum inform family members about what their child is learning, and contain ideas for activities to continue the learning at home and in the community.

Themes

The activities in *The Anti-Bullying and Teasing Book* are built around four themes—Community, Feelings, Friendship, and Teasing and Bullying. Each theme begins with background information, which is the framework for the activities, and a list of concepts that will be developed. The activities in Chapter 4, Community, set the tone and rules for a safe, caring, and welcoming environment; therefore, we strongly recommend doing those activities with children at the beginning of the school year. The activities in the other themes can be used throughout the school year in ways that best meet the needs of the group. We suggest reading through all the themes to get a sense of the whole. A brief description of each theme follows.

Community

This theme sets the tone for creating a sense of community or "family" in the classroom. Children learn the "whys" of rule-making and participate in creating rules for a friendly classroom and a friendly playground. Activities help children explore the commonalities and differences among class members and their families. Children bond together as they create a collage around familiar foods, including ethnic favorites enjoyed in their homes, and cooperate to build a class project from recyclables.

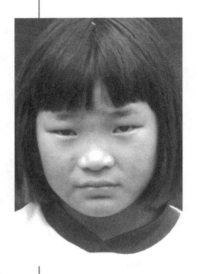

Feelings

Learning to understand feelings, one's own and others, is a big step in reducing teasing and bullying behavior. In this theme, children explore a full range of feelings, including anger, sadness, and exclusion as well as belonging and acceptance and gladness. Activities include stories and discussion, charting, reading and creating poems, singing songs of welcome, and a party.

Friendship

Typically, children come to school knowing the word, "friend," but have much to learn about the concepts that underlie the word. This theme helps children learn about the give and take, empathy, and sensitivity to others that are part of friendship. Through stories, puppets, and "new friend" activities, children gain experience with a wide range of concepts related to friendship.

Teasing and Bullying

This theme is designed to provide information and appropriate strategies to help young children cope with teasing and bullying situations that are present in virtually every preschool classroom. Teasing includes making fun of someone, calling names, using put-downs, or ridiculing another person. Bullying can take the form of repetitive physical, verbal, or psychological abuse—gesturing, hitting, pushing, shoving, insulting, or excluding.

Along with efforts to create a caring, safe, and welcoming environment for all children, it is important to address the issues of teasing and bullying in a proactive way. Through activities in this theme, children learn the difference between tattling and telling, the meaning of the terms teasing and bullying, that words can be as hurtful as physical pain, and the role of bystanders. They learn the importance of respecting cultures, preferences, and ideas that are different from their own.

Activities

The activities throughout the guide are literacy-based. Through class meetings, picture books, puppets, and simple role plays, children build developmentally appropriate literacy skills such as listening, discussion, vocabulary, word recognition, charting, graphing, and drawing. Each activity begins with the following information:

- **Setting:** Where the activity takes place (at a class meeting, in the dramatic play area, in the library area, or outdoors)
- **Materials:** What you will need to gather (picture book, chart paper, puppets, collage materials)
- **Time:** Approximate time to allow for each part of the activity
- **What Children Will Do:** The children's role in the activity (listen to a story and participate in a discussion, create a class book, participate in a cooperative game, and so on)
- **What Children Will Learn:** Social/emotional, cognitive, or other skills the activity will foster (cooperative play, new vocabulary, verbal expression)

The activities are formatted in numbered steps. Many activities are divided into two or three parts, each lasting about 15 minutes. Depending on your daily schedule and whether you have children for a half day or a full day, you can carry out the parts at different times of the day or spread them over several days. In some activities there are notes, which include teaching tips to make the activities go more smoothly.

Annotated Bibliography

Books are a key element in this guide. It is through picture books that children learn that other people also experience a broad range of positive and negative emotions as they enter a group situation. Books help to teach social strategies, empathy, cooperation, and how good it feels to be accepted and belong to a school community. Books lead to discussions that help children develop a myriad of literacy skills—listening, vocabulary, discussion, sound and word recognition. In addition, books expose children to art through the use of color and different styles of illustration or photography.

It is also a good idea to read through the Annotated Bibliography at the beginning of the year (see page 111). You will find books related to all four themes to select for the class library. The books in this bibliography have been carefully chosen to meet several criteria. They are well-written, represent a diverse group of children and families, depict girls and boys in nonstereotyped ways, are well-illustrated in a variety of art styles, teach about good character but are not "preachy," and are fun to read!

The bibliography also includes a selected list of books for adults. The books about teaching by Vivian Gussin Paley provide a philosophical approach to working with young children that was developed over many years spent working with preschoolers and kindergartners. Other titles provide background information on teasing and bullying in young children and activity guides to stimulate new ideas.

Conclusion

We urge you to use *The Anti-Bullying and Teasing Book* as a catalyst for making your classroom the caring, safe, and welcoming environment that all children deserve. As you conduct the activities, you will find strategies to make them work better for your particular school and classroom, and they will spark new ideas for activities. We urge you to act on these new ideas, adjusting them to your special teaching style. In other words, make them your own.

Enjoy the challenge!

CHAPTER 2

The Classroom Environment

Creating a caring classroom and school culture requires more than a series of activities. The caring philosophy must be reflected in every area of the learning environment. Setting up centers that affirm the values this book is designed to develop—empathy, sense of self and others, friendship, kindness, appropriate expression of feelings, acceptance and appreciation of difference—will convey to children that school is a caring, welcoming, and safe environment for all.

Circle or Meeting Times

Many of the activities in this book take place during circle or meeting times. When children are thinking about how to cooperate, when they are expressing their ideas and feelings about getting along or not getting along, and when they are sharing personal stories, the formation of the circle itself conveys a sense of trust and belonging. Circle or meeting times present opportunities to come together with children to share ideas, solve problems, read and discuss stories that promote pro-social behavior, and think about what needs to be done to strengthen the classroom community.

These gatherings can and should happen at different times during the day. A morning meeting is a time to personally welcome all the children with a song that mentions each person by name, for example, "A Hearty Welcome to You" (see page 61) and perhaps to share home events. A late morning gathering of children after work/play time can be an opportunity for a story and discussion. After a vigorous time out in the play yard or after a trip, a brief meeting can ease the transition to in-class activities. And, at the end of the day, it is important to get together to say "goodbye" to each other and to affirm that tomorrow everyone will be back together. The wonderful children's musician, Ella Jenkins, has songs that make every child feel welcome and included, and singing them at circle time helps to create a sense of classroom harmony.

"Let's Work It Out" Table

This is a place in the classroom where children can learn beginning negotiating skills and peaceful strategies for resolving differences. The "Let's Work It Out" table should be set up in a quiet area of the classroom, perhaps near the library or reading corner. If the table is near a wall, display some pictures of children in friendly poses and/or pictures of the beach or another calming nature scene. Have a box or basket on the table with some simple puppets representing boys, girls, and adults. The puppets can be made from wide craft sticks or felt, or they can be finger puppets—the simpler the better, so children can use them to represent a wide range of people and situations. As children gain experience using the table, they can create their own stick puppets, drawing on blank craft sticks with markers or crayons.

At first, you (or another adult) will need to sit with children and guide them through a process through which both sides of an incident can be aired. To introduce the idea to children:

1. Prepare a picture chart with the steps of the process (see next page).

   - Show two children sitting at the table; mark the picture Child A and Child B. **Note:** Use very simple stick figure drawings that can represent any child.
   - Show child A talking to child B.
   - Show child B talking to Child A. (These pictures will represent each child telling his or her side of the story.)
   - Show the children shaking hands with "We're friends again" written over the children.
   - Show an adult with the children.

2. Talk about the "Let's Work It Out" table at a class meeting. Explain that it is a place where children can go to talk about unfriendly situations that happen.
3. Ask everyone to come over to the table and look at the pictures and the puppets. Explain that you chose pictures that you thought would help children feel calmer and that, if they find it easier, they can talk over the problem through the puppets.
4. Go over the steps on the chart and explain that at first, and whenever else it is needed, a teacher will help children work out a solution.

1

2

3

4

5

5. Role play a situation that might be brought to the "Let's Work It Out" table. Frannie and Michelle are creating tall buildings in the block area. They both want to use the two arch-shaped blocks to make doorways. They refuse to share by each taking one block. Each girl says she needs two blocks. Both Frannie and Michelle are upset. Frannie yells, "I'm going to knock your building down." The teacher asks them to come with her to the "Let's Work It Out" table.

6. Ask the children if they have any ideas for working it out. For example:

   ● Each girl could use the two blocks for a certain amount of time, say 20 minutes each, or they could decide to share, each using one arch-shaped block.
   ● They could look for other blocks that would make good doorways (unit blocks can be combined to make many similar shapes).

7. Tell children that the "Let's Work It Out" table is another way to help the class solve problems without hurting each other.

"Let's Calm Down" Corner

Providing a space within the classroom where children can reduce feelings of tension or anger and remove themselves from teasing or other stressful situations will contribute to a climate of respect, trust, and safety. Strategies and props to help children calm down will build their sense of autonomy and ability to handle their emotions.

1. In a class meeting, read a story about something that comforts a child.
2. Ask children what kinds of things they do to comfort themselves. Do they hug a blanket, sit in a rocking chair, hold a favorite stuffed animal, look at picture books, or listen to music?
3. Explain that you would like to set up a "Let's Calm Down" corner in the classroom, a place where children can go if they are feeling angry or need some time away from others.

4. Ask children for ideas about what could go in the corner, for example a fish tank, tape/CD player, and earphones for listening to quiet music, stuffed animals, and books. You can suggest items such as pastel chalk and drawing paper, a basin of water and items for pouring, soft pillows, pictures of quiet Yoga exercises, playdough, and/or clay.

5. Together, look around the room for a good place to set up the corner.

6. Furnish the corner with the items the children have suggested, and others that you think are important.

7. When the corner is set up, make some rules together about how it should be used. For example:

- Tell the teacher you need to go to the area.
- Select what you want to do, for example, listen to music, hug a stuffed animal, or make a drawing.
- When you are ready to leave the area, put everything you have used back in place.

8. Create a picture chart of the rules for the "Let's Calm Down" corner (see sample illustrations), and hang it up in the area.

Dramatic Play Area

The dramatic play area is a place where children can role-play stories that further their understanding of the importance of showing empathy and kindness to others. Several activities in this book use puppets in the dramatic play area to act out teasing and bullying situations. In addition to these and the regular imaginative play that takes place in that area, you can suggest some new themes that relate to kindness for children to act out.

1. Before free play time, tell the children that you have an idea for today's dramatic play area. Ask, "If you were making up a play about how to make a new child feel welcome in our class, what would you do?"

2. As children put forth ideas, help shape them into a play scenario. You can suggest some embellishments to their ideas. The new child would need to know where to wash up, how to put things away at clean-up time, and how to sing the "Hearty Welcome" song (see page 61).

3. Ask if anyone would like to role-play the "new child" scene.

4. About once a week, offer an idea for a special dramatic play scenario that focuses on acts of kindness.

5. If you notice children making up similar scenarios on their own, be sure to acknowledge them at meeting time, so their kindness is affirmed.

Block Area

In addition to the wonderful role the block area plays in children's learning about math, science, and social studies, it can also be a place for building a sense of community in the classroom. The block area is a place to teach respect for space, one's own and others, and to practice skills for getting along, sharing, and resolving conflicts. When young children are constructing block buildings there are bound to be knockdowns, both on purpose and by accident, and these can cause hurt feelings, anger, and even physical hurts. Making rules with children for the block area can be very helpful.

1. On a day when there have been conflicts in the block area, call children together after clean-up time to talk about it.

2. Talk about how creating some rules will help make the area more enjoyable for everyone. Ask children to suggest some rules. If necessary, prompt their thinking with some questions:

- Do we need a rule that one person or group can't use all the blocks of one particular kind?
- What can we do if a building gets knocked over?
- How many children or groups can work comfortably at one time?

3. Create a chart of "Rules for the Block Area."
4. Revisit the rules from time to time.

Another way to create community in the Block Area is to create "New Friends" building groups. This is a technique for getting children to play with different people, and to get children who don't self-select block building to play in this important learning area. This is also a good technique for ensuring that girls and boys play together because they have much to learn from each other.

First, tell children that it is a "new friends" building day. Assign pairs or small groups of three or four children to work in the block area. Be prepared for some objections. Tell children your reasons for wanting them to work with new friends–to learn new ideas, to find out more about people in the class, to have fun in new ways.

Then, after the "new friends" building activity, ask a few children to report on what they constructed with their new friends.

Outdoor Play

Children need to run freely without restrictions, and the play yard is the place where that can happen. But using a piece of this time for games and exercises that build a sense of fair play and self-empowerment can help release energy in a positive way and create a sense of calm when children return to the classroom.

1. After children have had a sufficient time to let off steam, call everyone together for a "play fair" game. For example:

   - **Signal and Response**—Decide on a movement children will do when you clap your hands, for example, jump in place. Change the signal and response several times—you wave your hand and children tiptoe, you stamp your foot and they march in a circle. At first, you can make every change a separate game. When children have more experience, you can change the signal and cue their response without pausing.
   - **Freeze**—Form a circle and have children follow your movements, for example, move arms in a circle, stand on one leg, nod heads. At some point say, "freeze" and everyone has to stay in that position until you say, "unfreeze" and start another movement.

2. After the game, briefly describe what was different about it, for example, the game was fun but there were no winners or losers, everyone got to help someone else, and so on.
3. After the game, the children can return to free play.
4. Before returning to the classroom, call everyone together in a circle for some calming activities, such as yoga breathing and stretching exercises. Explain that this is a way of cooling down, much like athletes do after a run or a big game.
5. After the exercises, ask everyone to hold hands for a moment and stay quiet before returning to the classroom.

Conclusion

The preschool classroom presents an opportunity to be proactive about creating the learning environment we want to provide for children, and the human values we want to help them develop in their first school experience. To make the most of this opportunity we, as teachers, need to pay close attention to every aspect of our work and constantly re-examine the learning environment and the lessons we are imparting. One of the most gratifying aspects of preschool teaching is that you see your efforts clearly reflected in the well-being of the children.

CHAPTER 3

Family Involvement

Parents play a critical role in their children's education. A number of research studies have found that children whose parents participate in their education achieve more, have better attitudes toward school, and hold higher aspirations in life (Henderson et al, 2002). As the link between home and school at a time in children's lives when home-school communication is most frequent, you can actively demonstrate to parents that their participation matters.

It is important for families to know about classroom activities and goals for creating a caring community. You want and need their support. Likewise, parents need your support for their efforts in promoting care, kindness, and respect for others at home. Children benefit most when they receive similar messages at home and at school about pro-social behavior.

The letters included in this chapter provide a way for you to communicate with parents about what is happening in the classroom related to this curriculum. When you send the letters home, be sure to include information about the specific activities you are doing in your classroom. Take time to encourage families to read these letters and to do the suggested activities at home.

In addition to sending the letters, you can foster family partnerships around the creation of a caring community in many other ways:

- Create lines of open and ongoing communication—it's surprising how many parents feel uninformed about their child's daily experiences in the classroom.
- Talk with parents and other family members during informal drop-off or pick-up times about what they are doing at home.
- Plan a workshop so that parents can talk about the activities they are doing and share ideas for what works well.

- Create a "We Care for Each Other" bulletin board to display children's art and stories, and an "Acts of Kindness" bulletin board to keep track of kind acts at home and in school.
- Invite parents and other family members in to talk with the children about how they show their care for the community, for example, visiting a nursing home, coaching a Little League team, or bringing food to someone who has just had a baby.
- Set up a lending library of the books recommended in the bibliography (see page 111).
- Be sure that materials you send home are translated into the dominant language of children's families. Community or parent volunteers can be helpful in accomplishing this. Involve parents who speak both languages and use family partners if available.
- Create a newsletter or a website and encourage contributions from families as well as staff.

All of these activities will send the message that families are welcome and respected. Remember, children look to the important adults in their lives as role models of positive behavior.

Dear Family Members,

We are very pleased to tell you that our class is going to be engaged in a program designed to reduce teasing and bullying behavior and create a school climate that is safe, caring, and welcoming for every child. We'll learn important concepts of group interaction through activities that build language, social/emotional and interpersonal skills, small and large motor coordination, and cognitive development—all building blocks of good early childhood education.

In class, we'll be reading and discussing books that foster respect for oneself and others, that help children understand the ways that human beings are alike and different, and that teach the give and take of getting along in groups. Because living in families is such a vital part of young children's lives, we'll build on that to create a sense of family in our classroom.

Through the year, we'll be doing activities around four themes in this curriculum: Community, Feelings, Friendship, and Teasing and Bullying. At the start of each theme, you will receive a Family Letter with ideas for activities to do at home or in your community that will build on what we are doing in the classroom. The activities will be engaging and fun and, at the same time, will help children develop the skills that are important for success in school.

We look forward to working with you.

COMMUNITY THEME LETTER

Dear Family Members,

In school, we have been building a sense of community to help all the children feel that they belong. There are many home activities you can do to extend children's learning about what it means to be part of a community. We've listed some suggestions below, but we encourage you to think of your own ideas and share them with us.

- With your child, talk about the things your family does to help each other.
- Make a list of the things your child does (or can learn to do) to be helpful. Use pictures as well as words on the chart. Some suggestions might be to sort laundry, set the table, and pick up toys. Post the list on the refrigerator or other space at your child's eye level. Add to the list as you think of new ideas.
- Ask your child to tell you about the classroom rules she/he is helping to create. Can you make some rules for home, too? Decide together how to make and decorate a rules poster. Glitter is always a fun decoration.
- In school, we read a book written by kindergarten children, called *We Are All Alike...We Are All Different,* and we have made an "Alike and Different" class book. At home, you can make an "Alike and Different" family book. Together, draw pictures of family members. Show different types and colors of hair, size and shape, ages, favorite foods. While you are working, use comparison words such as *big, medium,* and *small* to describe sizes, *older* and *younger* to describe ages, and *curly, wavy,* and *straight* to describe hair. It's a fun way to build your child's vocabulary.
- You also can compare your family to a neighbor's family. How many people are in each family? Are there brothers and sisters in both? Do the neighbors have a pet? Do you?
- As a final activity for the Community theme, you will be asked to send some clean recyclables to school for a building project. The children will use masking tape to bind together boxes, tubes, and other objects into a large classroom structure. You can repeat this activity at home with your child and other family members. All it takes is some clean recyclables and masking tape. It's a lot of fun, and it teaches so many skills—cooperation, organization, large motor coordination, and symmetry and balance to name a few.

We hope you enjoy doing the home activities for the Community theme with your child.

Dear Family Members,

We hope you enjoyed doing activities with your child around the Community theme. Our classroom activities were fun and helped the children begin to feel that they were part of a school community. We will continue to create that sense of caring for each other as we move into activities around the Feelings theme.

You may already be hearing the "Hearty Welcome" song around the house. This simple song, sung to the tune of "Happy Birthday," promotes a sense of belonging and welcome, and we sing it every morning. Soon, we'll build some variations into the song but, for now, the children love singing it just as it is.

At school, we'll also talk about the opposite of feeling welcome. We'll explore what makes people feel unwelcome in school and in the community. Being left out of a game, saying unkind things, laughing at people, and not being invited to a party are all things that make children feel unhappy and excluded. Within the Feelings theme, we'll be building children's insights into their own feelings and those of others. There will be lots of discussion around charting of words that express feelings—glad, happy, mad, sad, angry, grouchy, scared—and puppet plays and stories to build understanding of these feelings. At home, you can extend the learning in many ways:

- Talk about feelings with your child—offer new words to help him/her express both positive and negative feelings
- Take a trip to the library to look for books about feelings. Talk about the feelings that are expressed in the pictures and words. Ask, "Did you ever feel this way?"
- Make a "kindness chart." Write down things your child does to help others, for example, comforts a crying baby or younger sibling, brings an older family member a drink or a newspaper, helps carry a package, pushes the swing for a baby in the park, or shares a toy.
- Play a "body talk" game. Express a feeling without using any words. For example, make an angry face and walk fast or make a sad face and walk slowly with your head down. Ask your child to guess the feeling. When the game feels familiar, ask your child if he/she would like to have a turn. Ask other family members to join the game.

Enjoy the Feelings theme with your child!

FRIENDSHIP THEME LETTER

Dear Family Members,

Once children enter preschool, having friends becomes a very important part of their daily lives. Children often ask to have play dates after school so they can extend their friendships beyond the school day. As children explore friendship, they will need to learn that it is a give-and-take process that doesn't always go smoothly. In school, we'll be using the theme of friendship to explore many aspects of what it means to be a friend. Learning to develop empathy, cooperate, and share are important parts of friendship.

You can help your child learn about the essence of friendship by doing activities at home. Here are some suggestions:

- Talk with your child about the friends he or she is making in school. Ask about how they play together. "Do you like to paint pictures, build with blocks, or work on puzzles?"
- Make a list of things friends do together such as sharing toys, making up games, and riding scooters or bicycles. Talk about the good feelings that come from being a friend.
- Take a trip to the library to look for books about friendship. Look up the words "friend" and "friendship" on the library computer to find titles.
- Think about some adults that your child is friendly with. Sometimes storekeepers or friends of an older sibling can act like a friend to a young child.
- Make a "friendship book." Your child can draw pictures of friends, or you can take photographs when friends come to play, and bind them into a book. Ask your child to say something about each picture and write it in the book.

Enjoy exploring friendships with your child!

Dear Family Members,

In our class, we have been talking about teasing and bullying—what it means, how it feels, and what to do about it. We want the classroom to be a place where children feel comfortable talking about this topic.

The children have created their own definitions for "teasing" and "bullying." They also have been learning about safe and age-appropriate ways to handle teasing and bullying situations. For example, children listen to short stories and choose strategies such as "walk away," "stand up for yourself," or 'get help." When we talk about the "stand up" strategy, we discuss ways to tell someone to stop doing or saying something that makes us uncomfortable, scared, or sad. We also talk about the importance of standing up for a friend and not being a bystander in teasing or bullying situations. When we talk about standing up for a friend, we also talk about doing it in a safe way. Children learn that they can remind the teaser about the classroom rules, they can use their words to try and stop the situation, or they can always ask an adult to help.

We hope you will encourage your child to talk about teasing and bullying at home, as well. Here are some ideas to get you started:

- Ask your child to tell you about the teasing and bullying activities she or he is doing in school.
- If your child has a difficult time talking about her or his feelings, you can help start the conversation by reading a book about teasing or bullying. Come by the classroom to see the books we are using, and/or take a trip to the library and ask the librarian for suggested titles.
- Use puppets, dolls, or stuffed animals to encourage your child to tell a story about teasing and bullying. Review the three strategies we have been discussing in class: walking away from the situation, standing up for yourself or a friend, or getting help from an adult.
- Have a discussion about teasing and bullying with other family members; sometimes, older siblings don't realize that they are teasing and bullying—they think they are just having fun.

Always affirm that teasing or bullying another person is not acceptable behavior. And remember that, as adults, we need to model the behavior we expect from our children.

CHAPTER 4

Community Theme

Background

If children feel good about themselves, they are less likely to engage in teasing and bullying behavior. You can help nurture a child's sense of self and belonging by building a caring and cooperative classroom community.

One of the first steps is to create a classroom "family." Children understand the concept of "family" when they enter preschool, even at age three. A child's family is her or his primary community, providing a first sense of belonging. Several activities in this section will help you further develop and nurture that sense of belonging by tapping into children's understanding of their own families and expanding it to their classroom experiences. The activities also foster respect for differences, which will help children become accepting and understanding members of their diverse school community. Several activities help children explore the concept of "alike and different." Through stories and discussions about physical features all human beings share, family structure, and favorite foods, children gain understanding about what people have in common, and appreciation for the ways in which we are different.

Many children entering preschool are having their first experiences in relating to children and adults outside their families. Creating and following rules are essential to the shaping of these experiences. It is important to remember, however, that children may have no knowledge of what rules are, and why they are important to school and community life. If we expect children to follow rules, they need to understand the reasons for having them, and be part of the process of creating them. It is important to do the rule-making activities for a friendly classroom and playground at the beginning of the school year, and to revisit them throughout the coming months.

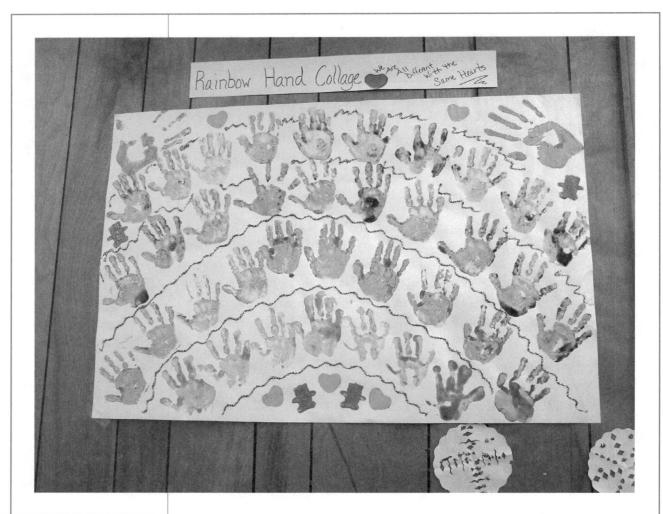

Rainbow Hand Collage — We Are All Different with the Same Hearts

- creating community
- cooperating
- respecting one's own and others' space
- sense of belonging
- sense of self
- sense of family
- alike and different

Through stories and discussions, puppet plays, and partnering activities, you can help children create a comfortable and respectful classroom community. Working together cooperatively by making collages and engaging in building activities helps children bond as a group. Ultimately, they will understand how their behavior can positively and negatively affect their community.

ACTIVITY

Helping Each Other at Home and at School

What Children Will Do

Discuss aspects of family life

Compare being helpful at home and in school

What Children Will Learn

What the word *helpful* means

How people help each other in families and in school

Setting

Class meeting

Materials

- Chart paper
- Magazines
- Markers

Time

Part One–15 min.
Part Two–15 min.

A key vocabulary word in this lesson is *helpful*. Children may understand the concept but not know the word. If you have a helpers list for classroom jobs, you can show children that the first part of the word is the same, and explain that when we do something like putting away the toys or watering the plants, we are being *helpful*. Before doing the lesson, start using the word, "helpful." For example, during another part of the day when children are doing their jobs you might say, "Everyone is being so helpful today." Or, if a child comforts another child who is hurt, you might say, "Bringing Josh a glass of water when he fell down was a very helpful thing to do."

Before Getting Started

Use the marker to divide the chart paper into two columns, one side headed "Helpful at Home" (illustrated by a picture cut from a magazine of a child helping an adult at home) and the other "Helpful at School" (illustrated by a photograph of a child or children doing a classroom job).

Part One

1. During class meeting, show children the chart you have prepared and briefly describe the discussion topic. You might say, "I've been thinking about our class and how many ways it is like a family. Families do things to help each other, and in school we also do things to help each other."

2. Ask children to think about what it means to be a member of a family. List their ideas on the "Helpful at Home" side of the chart paper. Ask questions as needed to spur the discussion:

- What is something you like about being in a family?

- What do you do to be helpful in your family (set the table, put your toys away, get dressed by yourself, be quiet when someone is resting)?
- Is it a good feeling to be helpful?

3. After you have listed the children's thoughts say, "Later on today (or tomorrow if you have a half-day schedule), we'll think about some of the helpful things we do in our classroom."

Part Two

1. Briefly remind children of the things they listed on the "Helpful at Home" chart.
2. Tell children that now they are going to make a "Helpful at School" chart.
3. List children's ideas on the classroom side of the chart. Together think about some helpful ways that children can act in the classroom:

- put the toys and materials away together
- help someone who is having a problem or a difficult day
- be nice to each other
- act kindly
- respect each other's feelings

4. Point out the similarities between being helpful at home and helpful at school.

Note: Another way to do this activity is to encourage children to create collages that show children being helpful at home, in school, and in the community. For this activity, you will need a variety of pictures cut from magazines and catalogs and some large pieces of poster board. It may be best to divide the class into groups of four to six children and give each group a task, for example, "home helpers," "school helpers," and "community helpers."

ACTIVITY

Rules for a Friendly Classroom

What Children Will Do

Create a set of rules for the classroom

What Children Will Learn

Social/emotional skills

How to cooperate

Setting

Class meeting

Materials

- Large sheet of construction paper
- Drawing paper
- Tape
- Crayons/markers

Time

Part One–15 min.
Part Two–20 min.

Part One

1. Find out what children know about rules. Ask, "Does anyone have an idea about what the word *rule* means?" If no one responds, continue to ask questions to spur children's thinking. For example, say, "Do you have to go to bed at a certain time? Do you have to put your toys away? Do you have to hold a grownup's hand when you cross the street?" Explain that these are rules that help to teach children to be healthy, responsible, and safe.

2. Ask children to help think of rules for the classroom that will make it a friendly place for everyone. Prompt children with questions about key areas that need rules. For each area, ask them to think about the consequences of not having a rule. As the children talk, write down their rules and reasons.

   - Do we need a rule about hanging up our coats? What would happen if we just left them on the floor?
   - Do we need a rule about listening during meeting time and story time? Why?
   - Do we need a rule about how to use our hands and bodies so they don't hurt anybody? Why?
   - Do we need a rule about putting toys and materials away at clean-up time? Why?
   - Do we need a rule about treating each other kindly? What would happen if we didn't do that?

3. Say that you will write all the rules the children have suggested on a big piece of paper and that later (or tomorrow) they will make pictures about the rules.
   Note: You can also write each rule on a sentence strip, which would allow more flexibility in adding and eliminating rules throughout the year.

Part Two

1. Give out drawing paper and crayons. While children are drawing, write their rules (in their own language) in the center of a large piece of construction paper (or on sentence strips). Let children attach their drawings around the edge to decorate the "Rules for a Friendly Classroom" poster.

RULES

1. Walk.

2. Take care of our friends.

3. Take care of our toys and our classroom.

2. Mount the poster on the wall, and read it aloud before the children leave for the day.

3. Revisit the rules frequently. Add new rules (or eliminate rules) as needed and remind children of the reasons for having rules.

Rules for a Friendly Playground

What Children Will Do	**What Children Will Learn**
Create a set of rules for the play area	Social/emotional skills How to cooperate

Setting

Play area or yard

Materials

- Large piece of construction paper
- Drawing paper
- Crayons

Time

Part One–15 min.
Part Two–20 min.

This rule-making activity should be done outdoors on a nice day at the beginning of the school year. You may want to let children play freely for a while to release their energy before you call them together.

Part One

1. Ask children to sit in a circle. If you have large blocks, you can have two children share a block. They also can sit around the edge of the sandbox or on the grass or a blanket.

2. Remind children about the "Rules for a Friendly Classroom" poster they made and ask the children to remember what rules they made. Suggest that they make another poster called "Rules for a Friendly Playground."

3. Ask questions to spur children's thinking about what rules are needed for the playground.

   - What are some rules we need to make our playground safe and pleasant for everyone?
   - Why do we need to be careful when we're running? When we're climbing?
   - How can we make sure every person is enjoying outdoor time?
   - Suppose we want to use a sand toy and someone else has it?

Part Two

1. Back in the classroom or in an outdoor meeting area, create a poster of "Rules for a Friendly Playground." Show children the large piece of construction paper and give out the drawing paper and crayons. As in the classroom poster, write the rules in the center and let children tape their drawings around the edge.

2. Mount the poster on the door leading out to the play area.

ACTIVITY

Alike and Different Story and Chart

Setting

Class meeting area, library corner, or other designated area for storytelling

Materials

- *We Are All Alike...We Are All Different** by the Cheltenham Elementary School kindergartners
- Chart paper and markers

Time

Part One—15 min.
Part Two—15 min.

*This book was written and illustrated by kindergartners, with supplementary photographs, to celebrate the commonalities and differences that symbolize American diversity.

What Children Will Do

Listen to a story

Explore concepts of alike and different

What Children Will Learn

Vocabulary

Comparison

Part One

1. Read the title of the story. Ask children if they know what the word *alike* means. Help them discover the meaning by looking at the children on the cover. Is everyone's skin color the same? Are they all boys? Girls? As soon as someone uses the word *same,* explain that alike is another word for same.

2. Ask, "Can anybody guess who wrote this story?" If children don't guess, tell them it was written by children in kindergarten.

3. Read the story.

4. Talk about the main story points.

Part Two

1. With the children, make an "Alike and Different" chart. Start with the ways that people are alike, for example, we all have eyes, ears, hair, arms, legs, fingers, toes. Then list the ways we can be different, for example, color of eyes, skin, and hair; size; weight; languages we speak; foods we eat. Let children come up with as many suggestions as they can think of, and then ask questions to spur their thinking further:

   - Do all people speak the same language? What language does your family speak at home?
   - Let's think about the different kinds of homes people live in.
   - Do all people eat the same kind of food? What special foods do people in your family eat?
   - Is everyone's skin the same color?
   - Does everyone have a pet? What are the different kinds of pets that live with families?

2. Read the entire chart aloud.

ALIKE	DIFFERENT
We all play with toys.	Our clothes are different colors.
We all have hair.	Some of us are boys.
We all have hands.	Some of us are girls.
We all have bodies.	We wear different colored shoes.
We all have eyes.	
We all wear shoes.	
We all have hearts.	

3. Hang up the "Alike and Different" chart in the meeting area or at the "Let's Work It Out" Table.

    Note: As an alternative activity, encourage the children to create an "Alike and Different" mural for the classroom. After the discussion, group children around a large piece of brown wrapping paper (be sure each child has a comfortable space around the edge of the paper). Cut pictures of many diverse adults and children from magazines and catalogs; be sure to include all kinds of family groups and adults and children with disabilities in the collection. Put the pictures in several baskets so children don't have to reach very far to make their selections. Provide glue sticks and markers in case some children want to draw a picture of their own on the mural. If pets are part of the discussion, you can add a variety of pets to the selection.

    Another alternative activity is to have children create "alike and different" stick puppets. Either cut circles or give each child two small paper plates. Ask children to draw "someone like me" depicting their own skin tone, hair color, and eye color. On the second plate or circle, ask children to draw "someone different from me" again thinking about skin tone, hair color, and eye color. Attach the "alike" picture on one side of a craft stick and the "different" picture on the other side.

Alike	Different
 everyone sleeps	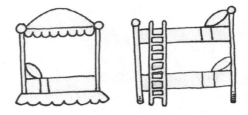 we have different beds
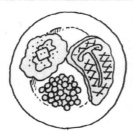 everyone eats	 we like different foods
 everyone plays	 we play different games
everyone loves	 we love different people

ACTIVITY
Alike and Different Families

What Children Will Do	**What Children Will Learn**
Listen to a story	Fine motor skills
Talk about their family structure	Vocabulary
Draw pictures of their family	

Setting
Meeting area with table and chairs (for drawing)

Materials
- Alike and Different chart (from activity on page 46)
- *We Are All Alike…We Are All Different* by the Cheltenham Elementary School kindergartners
- Drawing paper
- Skin-tone crayons
- Individual folders for each child

Time
Part One–15 min.
Part Two–20 min.

Part One

1. At meeting time, briefly review the "Alike and Different" chart, and read the section on families in *We Are All Alike…We Are All Different*. Tell children that they are going to make a picture of their family and talk about how their families are alike and different.

2. Give out drawing paper and skin-tone crayons. As children draw, walk around and write the names of family members on their pictures. You may want to prompt children to think about adding a grandmother, other relative, or significant adult that you know is close to the child. Encourage the use of skin-tone crayons that approximate the child's own skin. If it is different from his or her family's skin tone, help the child choose colors for both.

3. Give the children folders to hold their drawings and ask them to make a design on the folder so they will recognize it later. (Also write each child's name on the folder just in case they forget which design was theirs.)

Part Two

1. Look at the children's pictures and ask them to talk about the family members they have drawn.

2. After everyone has had a turn to describe the pictures, sum up the things that are alike and different in each. Following are some examples. Use your knowledge of the children in your class to decide what points to make. Be sure to make a closing point that what is the same is that families love each other and take care of children.

   - Some of us have brothers and sisters.
   - Some of us are the only child in our family.
   - Some of us live with our grandparents.
   - Some of our families have a mommy and daddy, some a mommy, some a daddy, some two mommies or daddies.
   - All of our families have people that love and take care of each other.

3. Ask children to put their family pictures in their folders. Explain that they are going to talk about their pictures again on another day.

ACTIVITY

Family Sharing

What Children Will Do
Share information about their family with a partner and the class

What Children Will Learn
Vocabulary
How to work in pairs
How to share information

Setting
Work tables and meeting area

Materials
- Cards with partners' names
- Children's folders with family drawings

Time
20 min.

Before Getting Started
Think about the makeup of your group and create a list of pairs. Print the names of each pair on a card. Try to match up children who will work well together. For example, you might pair a shy child with one who is more outgoing or put a child who needs help with a child who likes to help others. When thinking about the pairs, mix boys and girls and try to partner children who are not already regular playmates in the classroom.
Note: If your class will not divide evenly, think of the children who can work well in a group of three and print all three names on one card.

1. Introduce the concept of pairs. Ask children if anyone has an idea about what the word *pair* means. If no one can clearly define what that means, explain that when two people work together we call them a pair. Also tell children that the word we use to describe two of anything is *pair* (shoes, socks, earrings, and so on). You may also need to explain that there are some children who will work on the activity as a group of three, or a *threesome*.
2. Call out the names of the pairs (and/or threesomes) and put their cards on the table where they will sit. Say, "Now we are going to do something new with our family pictures. First, I'm going to give you back your family picture. Then you show the picture to your partner and tell her or him about your family."
3. As children tell their partner(s) about their families, circulate to see if they need any help. Be sure that everyone has a turn. Some children may be too shy or afraid to talk about their families. If this is the case, you may want to sit next to the child and ask if you can help. You could ask the child if it would be all right for you to tell something that you know about the child's family, or ask if the child would like to use puppets, or select pictures from a pile you provide, instead.

4. Ask pairs of children to come up and share what they learned about each other's family. If there is a threesome, ask each child to tell about one other family (be sure each family is represented).

5. Summarize what was shared so children come away from the activity with a sense that they are part of a community of families.

6. Ask children to put their family pictures back in their folders. Explain that they will make other pictures that will become part of a family book.

Make a Family Book

What Children Will Do	**What Children Will Learn**
Draw pictures of their pets, favorite foods, and home	Fine motor skills
Make a class book	Vocabulary

Setting

Meeting area with table and chairs (for drawing)

Materials

- Children's individual folders and family pictures
- Drawing paper
- Crayons

Time

Class meetings and drawing activities over several days for 15 min. per activity

Part One

1. At meeting time, briefly review the previous discussions children have had about their families. Tell children that they are going to make a book about their families for the class library. Talk about what should be in the book, for example, pictures of everyone's family, pets, foods, home.
Note: This drawing activity can take place over several days.

2. Give out drawing paper and crayons.

3. Ask children to draw pictures for the family book:

   - **Pets:** If a child does not have a pet, she or he can draw an imaginary one, or one they would like to have. As children work, circulate to write down the names of their pets.
   - **Food:** The foods can be something that their family likes to eat, or the child's favorite food.
   - **Home:** Children can draw pictures of their homes (house, apartment, trailer) or of individual rooms (bedroom, kitchen, living room).
   Note: Be prepared for what the children may draw. For example, some children may live in a shelter.

4. Be sure that children put their names on their drawings.

Part Two

1. After all the pictures are finished, bind them into a book (if laminating equipment is available, the book will last longer). There are several ways to make a class book out of children's drawings: punch three holes in the papers along the left margin and lace a shoelace through the holes; or put paper fasteners or rings through the holes; or punch one hole in the upper left corner of the papers and use a loose-leaf ring to bind them.

2. Read the class book during story time. Put the book in the class library, and be sure to re-read it often during the school year. If a family situation changes during the year or a new pet joins the family, you can ask the child to make a new page for the book.

ACTIVITY
Our Favorite Foods Collage

Setting
Meeting time and floor or work tables

Materials
- *We Are All Alike... We Are All Different* by the Cheltenham Elementary School kindergartners
- Chart paper and markers for graph
- Large paper for class collage
- Pictures of various foods cut from newspapers, food circulars, and magazines (try to have several types of ethnic foods and several copies of each type of food)
- Baskets or trays to hold the collage pieces
- Glue sticks

Time
Part One—15 min.
Part Two—20 min.

What Children Will Do
Create an "Our Favorite Foods" graph and collage

What Children Will Learn
Fine motor skills
Graphing skills
Vocabulary
How to use descriptive language
How to show respect for others

Part One
1. Briefly remind children about the Alike and Different discussion (see pages 46-48), and review the two pages on foods in *We Are All Alike...We Are All Different*. Can children name the foods that the children ate in the book?
2. Ask children to tell you about their favorite kind of food. As children talk, write the name of the food across the bottom of chart paper in a column, and ask each child to pick one of the magazine pictures to illustrate, for example, ice cream, pizza, macaroni and cheese, sushi, and spaghetti. Then ask the children to raise their hands to vote on each choice, and make an "Our Favorite Foods" graph.
3. With children, count aloud the number of "votes" for each food. Ask, "Which food has the highest number? That is the favorite food of the group."

Part Two
1. Set up the collage space and materials. Usually the floor is a comfortable space when many children need to work together. If the class is large, you can divide the group in half or thirds and mark off one area of the paper for each group. Write the title, "All Kinds of Food," in the center of the paper in large letters.
2. Talk about all the different kinds of food people eat. Show the children a few samples of the cutouts for the collage, emphasizing the different kinds of food and the cultures they represent.
3. Let children select pictures and glue them onto the collage paper. If you are doing the activity as a whole group, place the baskets and glue sticks in several places to provide easy access. If you are dividing the group into smaller groups, place the materials in the area you have marked off for the group. Either way, make sure that each child has a specific place to work. Remind children about being respectful of each person's workspace.

Note: This activity can take place over several days.

4. As the children work, you can write the names of the foods with a marker.

5. When the collage is finished, invite the children sit around the edge and talk about their work. Use the discussion as an opportunity to work on vocabulary skills. Ask questions about the colors and shapes of the foods. Point to a picture and ask if anyone has eaten that food. Can they describe how it tastes? How does it smell?

6. If you have been discussing various food groups, try to put the food pictures on the collage into the proper food groups. You may want to put a colored letter in a circle next to each picture—D for dairy, V for vegetable, M for meat, F for fruit, and so on.

7. With the children, decide where to hang the collage.

Our Favorite Foods	
hamburger	6
pizza	5
ice cream	3
taco	2
macaroni and cheese	1

Getting Ready to Build

Setting
Class meeting

Materials
- A few recyclables such as cereal boxes, shoeboxes, empty paper towel and gift paper rolls
- Chart paper and markers for writing a class letter to families
- Classroom calendar

Time
10 min. for planning, 15 min. for writing a letter to families

What Children Will Do
Plan and write a letter to families

What Children Will Learn
Vocabulary
How to plan an activity
How to write a letter

1. At a class meeting explain to the children that they will do a building project as a class. Explain that they will build a structure using "recyclables." Stress the fact that everyone will be working together on this project.

2. Ask children if they know the meaning of the word, "recycle." Do they recycle garbage/trash where they live? Explain that things that go into the recycling bin at home are called "recyclables." Have a few sample recyclables ready, for example, a cereal box, shoebox, paper towel tubes, and gift paper rolls.

3. Tell children that everyone will need to gather recyclables for the building project. Ask children how they think they could gather the materials for the structure. If no one mentions it, suggest asking family members to send items to school.

4. Together, make a list of the items needed. On large chart paper, write a letter using children's words to ask families to save clean recyclables and send them to school. Look at the class calendar and choose a date when all the materials should be returned to school (It should take about one week to gather enough items).

5. Transfer the letter onto letter-size paper and send it home with each child.
   Note: Remind families to send in recyclables throughout the week. Be sure to gather a fair amount yourself to ensure that there is enough building material.

6. While the class is gathering materials, use the class calendar to mark off each day until it's time to build.

A Class Building Project

What Children Will Do

Sort recyclables

Plan and build a communal structure using recyclables and masking tape

What Children Will Learn

How to plan as a group

How to sort

Small and large motor skills

Cooperation

Setting

The block area or other large space in the classroom

Materials

- Collected recyclables (see activity on previous page) such as one large, sturdy carton, cereal boxes, shoeboxes, empty paper towel tubes and gift paper rolls, small gift boxes, round cartons (bread crumbs, oatmeal)
- Interesting shapes such as candy or cookie box dividers, plastic berry boxes
- Several rolls of masking tape

  Note: If possible, obtain a camera to photograph children with their finished product.

Time

Part One–20 min.

Part Two–15 min.

Part One

1. Bring everyone together and explain that people will work in small groups to build a structure, and these structures will be joined into one big structure at the end.

2. Assign groups of children to sort the recyclables:

   - **Group A**—puts all the cereal and shoeboxes in a pile
   - **Group B**—collects all the rolls and tubes in a pile
   - **Group C**—collects all the small boxes and other small objects
   - **Group D**—collects miscellaneous items

   Note: There may not be a need for a Group D

3. Assign each group a work area and place strips of masking tape nearby.
4. Tell children that each group will need to use a certain amount from each pile to make a structure. (The number of items will depend on how many recyclables have been collected.) Each group could start by selecting two items from each pile, and then take one more until all the items are used.
5. Tell the children that they need to plan together before they start their structure. You will need to demonstrate how to use the tape strips so that they join two items together.
6. As children work, visit each group to make sure that everyone is participating.
7. Save all the small structures in a safe place.

Part Two
1. Bring the small structures together into a new area (you may need to do some additional taping to make them secure). Ask the children how the structures should go together. Should it be very tall? Should it be long like a train? (You may want to suggest this, since a tall structure would require standing on chairs or a lot of adult help.)
2. Join the structures together. If you and the class decide to make a tall structure, show the children that putting a large carton on the bottom as a base will make the structure much more secure.
3. Take a picture of all the children standing around their structure!
4. If possible, display the structure in the school hallway, lunchroom, or any space where other children and parents can see it.

CHAPTER 5

Feelings Theme

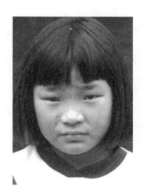

Background

Setting a tone of welcome can go a long way toward building a classroom culture of warmth and acceptance, which will minimize teasing, taunting, and other negative behaviors. Starting each day with a "welcome song," and greeting children by saying "welcome" and "good morning" will help to create a positive classroom environment. Unfortunately, certain behaviors can mar children's sense of belonging and make them feel unwelcome in school. The activities in this section provide you with many ways to explore with children what it means and how it feels to be welcome and unwelcome.

It is important to acknowledge children's negative feelings as well as their positive ones. Through stories, poems, puppet plays, writing, and drawing, you will be able to help children understand that everyone experiences a range of emotions—from glad to sad to mad.

It is critical to help children begin to develop insight into and empathy for the feelings of others. Four-year-olds are egocentric; they know how it feels to them when they are happy, sad, hurt physically or emotionally, angry, or frightened. Yet, often they do not understand the effect of these feelings on others or the role they themselves play in creating positive or negative feelings in other children. Even preschoolers can exhibit hurtful behaviors such as exclusion, ostracism, and name-calling. While four-year-olds may not know the word *exclusion,* they do know how hurt they feel when they are left out of a group. Several of the activities help children talk about how they feel when they are left out and to understand that to leave someone else out is to hurt them on purpose.

- feelings (one's own and others')
- self-awareness
- empathy
- friendship
- belonging
- kindness
- exclusion

People communicate their feelings in many different ways—through language, by touching others, by withdrawing, and through body language. We all recognize an angry walk, a happy walk, a frightened walk, or a sad walk. Young children, however, are not always sensitive to their own body language or that of their classmates. Building awareness of the messages conveyed through body language can help children develop empathy, caution, and increased understanding of themselves and others.

"I Feel Welcome" Song and Chart

What Children Will Do
Explore what makes them feel welcome in school

What Children Will Learn
Vocabulary

How to make their classmates feel welcome

Setting
Class meeting or circle time

Materials
- Chart paper
- Markers

Time
Part One–15 min.
Part Two–15 min.

Part One

1. Create a "welcome song" that you can sing at the start of each day. For example, you can use the tune of "Happy Birthday".

   A hearty welcome to you, a hearty welcome to you,
   A hearty welcome, dear children, a hearty welcome to you.

   This can also be sung using each child's name on the third line, for example, "a hearty welcome, dear Mary."
   Note: Singing the welcome song is an effective way to make children feel welcome after they have been away or absent due to illness.

2. After children are comfortable with the words to the welcome song, vary the song to reflect different aspects of each child, for example:

   A hearty welcome to you, a hearty welcome to you,
   A hearty welcome, dear Daniel, today you are wearing blue.

3. After children are familiar with the variations of the welcome song, you can pause on the last line, and they can make up a last line for themselves.

Part Two

1. At class meeting or circle time, ask children what they think the word *welcome* means. If needed, use some prompting questions to get the discussion going.

   - Do you think *welcome* is a happy word?
   - Have you heard me say, "Welcome" to you in the morning?
   - Am I smiling when I say it?
   - How do you feel when we sing the welcome song?

2. When children have an understanding of the word, make a chart of the things that make them feel welcome in school. For example:

- when someone wants to play with me
- when someone says they like me
- when someone says you are my friend
- when my teacher smiles and says, "Welcome" to me in the morning

I FEEL WELCOME...

When people share their show and tell

When I color with my friends

When I play cars

When my friend reads me a book

When my friends are near me on their mats

When I am asked to be a helper

3. Encourage younger children to demonstrate ways to show that another child is welcome, for example, give a friend a hug, take a friend's hand and go to a play area, or smile and say, "Hi."
4. Hang the chart at children's eye level in the meeting area or near the "Let's Work It Out" table.
   Note: A chart can use pictures as well as words.

"I Feel Welcome" Poem

What Children Will Do
Create a rhyming poem with a welcome theme

What Children Will Learn
Vocabulary
How to construct a poem
How to rhyme

Setting
Class meeting or circle time

Materials
- "I Feel Welcome" chart
- Glue sticks
- Decorations (sparkles, sequins, collage scraps)

Time
15 min.

1. Briefly remind children of their discussion about the word *welcome*, and read the "I Feel Welcome" chart.

2. Ask children if they would like to make a welcome poem for their class. Read the following poem to help them understand how a poem sounds. In addition, recite a few familiar songs that rhyme, such as "Twinkle, Twinkle, Little Star" or "Row, Row, Row Your Boat."

   My Shadow by Robert Louis Stevenson
   I have a little shadow that goes in and out with me,
   And what can be the use of him is more than I can see.
   He is very, very like me from the heels up to the head;
   And I see him jump before me, when I jump into my bed.

   The funniest thing about him is the way he likes to grow.
   Not at all like proper children, which is always very slow.
   For he sometimes shoots up taller like an India-rubber ball,
   And he sometimes gets so little that there's none of him at all.

3. Explore possible rhyming words—for example, block, clock, sock; or ball, tall, and call. Then, try to make up a poem of your own. (See sample poem on the next page).

4. Write the poem on a large sheet of poster paper, and encourage the children to decorate it with collage scraps, sparkles, sequins, and so on.

5. Hang the class welcome poem next to their "I Feel Welcome" chart.

I FEEL WELCOME...

When everyone says, "Good morning," to me,

It makes me happy as can be.

When I am asked to be a helper,

I am glad to be the helper.

When my friends share their toys,

I feel the pocket of Corduroy.

When my friends are near me on their mat,

I'm as happy as can be.

When I play with my friends in Home Living,

There is lots of sharing and giving.

When people share their show-and-tell,

I like to be their friend as well.

"I Feel Unwelcome" Chart

What Children Will Do

Discuss the meaning of
welcome/unwelcome
Create a chart

What Children Will Learn

Vocabulary
What the word *opposite* means
How their behavior affects others

Setting

Class meeting

Materials

- "I Feel Welcome" chart and welcome poem
- Markers

Time

Part One–10 min.
Part Two–15 min.

Part One

1. Remind children of the discussions they have had about feeling welcome in school. Sing your welcome song, and read the "I Feel Welcome" chart and the class welcome poem aloud.

2. Ask children if they have an idea about what the word *unwelcome* means. You may need to prompt the discussion:

   - What would it feel like to be unwelcome?
   - Would that be a happy feeling?
   - Let's compare the word *unwelcome* with the words on our chart.

3. Introduce the word *opposites*. Ask children if they know what it means. Give a few examples, such as open/close, up/down, asleep/awake. Discuss how the words *welcome* and *unwelcome* are opposites.

Part Two

1. Read each positive statement on the "I Feel Welcome" chart, and have children make up an opposite statement for the "I Feel Unwelcome" chart. For example:

   I Feel Welcome
   - When someone wants to play with me
   - When someone tells me they like me
   - When someone says, "You are my friend"
   - When my teacher smiles and says, "Welcome," to me in the morning

I Feel Unwelcome

- When someone says I can't play
- When someone says, "You're not my friend"
- When someone makes a face at me
- When someone calls me a bad name

2. Compare the feelings that each chart generates.
3. Close the discussion on a positive note by reviewing the happier feelings on the "I Feel Welcome" chart.
4. Tell children that everyone needs to work to make the classroom a welcoming place.

ACTIVITY
Feeling Left Out

What Children Will Do
Respond to a puppet play about exclusion

What Children Will Learn
Social/emotional skills
Empathy
Problem-solving skills

Setting
Circle (children can sit on a rug or on small chairs arranged in a circle)

Materials
- Puppets

Time
20 min.

1. Ask children to sit in a circle on the floor or on chairs.
2. Use the puppets to role play the following story:

   Freddy and Jake are in the yard. Freddy says, "Go away, Jake. You can't play in my special game." Jake asks, "Why can't I?" Freddy says," 'Cause I say so." Jake hangs his head and goes away.

3. Ask children how they think Jake feels. Does he feel happy? Sad? Angry? Have they ever felt this way?
4. Ask children what they think Jake should do. What would happen if:

   - Jake told Freddy that his feelings are hurt
   - Jake pretends he doesn't care about playing with Freddy

5. Ask children if anyone would like to use the puppets to act out what they think Jake could do. If no one volunteers, you can use the puppets to demonstrate.

Party Glad...Party Sad

Setting
Library area

Materials
- *Feelings* by Aliki

Time
15-20 min.

What Children Will Do
Listen to a short happy birthday story and think about a sad one

What Children Will Learn
Social/emotional skills

What it feels like to be included and excluded

1. Tell children that today you want them to think more about how they feel when they are left out.
2. Read page 7 of *Feelings*. Ask children how they know the boy is feeling happy.
   Note: The illustrations in this book are very small, so be sure to pass it around so that every child can see them.
3. Tell the children that there is more to the birthday story. Read pages 26 and 27 and talk about all the happy and friendly feelings in the story.
4. Ask children to think about these questions:

   - What if Alfred didn't invite Bob to his party?
   - How do you think Bob would feel? Would he feel happy? Sad?
   - Would he create such a nice present?

5. Summarize the discussion. Tell children that no one feels happy when they are left out. Ask children to agree that in their classroom no one should ever feel left out, and then add that to your list of class rules.

Class Party

What Children Will Do

Plan a party, make an invitation, and invite a classmate

What Children Will Learn

Vocabulary

Social/emotional skills

How to make an invitation

Setting

Worktables

Materials

- Paper
- Markers or crayons

Time

Part One–15 min. (to make invitation)

Part Two–15-20 min. (for class party)

Before Getting Started

Write each child's name on an 8 ½ x 11 piece of paper, fold it in half, and put all the papers in a basket or bowl.

Part One

1. Explain that the children are going to help plan a class party for the next day at snack time and that each child will send an invitation to a classmate. Ask children:

   - Should we decorate the room for the party? How?
   - Should we make place mats?
   - Should we have a special snack? Talk about healthy snack possibilities.

2. Have each child pick a name from the bowl. Explain that they will invite this classmate to the party. Then encourage the children to draw a picture on the paper as an invitation to the party. Help each child sign his or her name to the drawing.

Part Two

1. The next day, have children hand out their invitations at circle time. Ask children to describe how they felt when they received the invitation.
2. Decorate for the party.
3. Enjoy the party!
4. Have a brief discussion after the party. Talk about how good it felt to be invited by a classroom friend and to celebrate together.

ACTIVITY

Feeling Words

Setting
Class meeting or circle time

Materials
- Chart paper
- Markers
- 2 hand puppets

Time
Part One—10 min.
Part Two—15 min.
Part Three—10 min.

What Children Will Do
Generate a list of words related to feelings

Watch the teacher demonstrate the words using hand puppets

What Children Will Learn
Vocabulary
Social/emotional skills
Empathy

Part One

1. Have children arrange themselves in a circle on the floor or on chairs. Ask each child to hold the hand of the child on either side of them. Count to ten, and then ask them to drop hands. Help children understand that the hand-holding was a way to help them feel connected to each other.

2. Explain that another way to be connected to each other is to learn about the feelings we share. Ask children if they know the meaning of the word *feelings*. Move the discussion forward with questions:

   - Is happy a feeling?
   - Can someone tell us what it feels like when you are happy?
   - Is sadness a feeling?
   - Can someone tell us what makes us feel sad?
   - What makes us feel angry?

3. Write all the feelings children think of on chart paper. In addition, children can make "feelings" drawings on paper plates. Give out plates and ask children to draw faces on them that look happy, sad, angry, and scared.

sad   angry   happy   scared

Children can talk about their feelings by holding the plate with the appropriate expression up to their own faces.

Part Two

1. Read the "Feelings" chart aloud. Explain that you are going to use puppets in little plays about the feelings children listed on the chart. Play out some brief "feeling scenarios" with the puppets. For example, one scenario could be: I am happy to have a friend play with me. Ask the children to show how they look when they are happy. Continue with other feelings, including sad, angry, and scared.

2. Point out a few examples: "Daniel looks very sad when he hangs his head down and we can't see his eyes." "Sharon's face was red when she showed that she was angry." "Marie was shaking when she was scared."
    Note: The puppet plays can take place over several days or with small groups of children in the dramatic play area.

Part Three

1. Remind children of the puppet plays about feelings. Replay the sad and angry scenes.

2. Ask children what they think they could do if they saw someone in the class who was feeling sad or angry. How could they help that person to feel better? What could they do if someone looked very unhappy? Act out their suggestions with the puppets, for example, make a comforting gesture.

3. Remind children that we all have many feelings, and we can help each other to feel better when we are sad or angry. We can also share in each other's happy feelings. Ask children to hold hands again so everyone can feel connected.

Feeling Grouchy

Setting
Library area

Materials
- *The Grouchy Ladybug* by Eric Carle
- Markers
- Chart paper

Time
Part One–15 min.
Part Two–15 min.

What Children Will Do
Listen to a story

Talk about feeling grouchy and angry, and how they can calm down

What Children Will Learn
Vocabulary

How to help themselves when they are feeling grouchy or angry

This classic story by Eric Carle, a favorite of all children, provides opportunities to talk about feelings, especially anger, and can lead to extended lessons about how we treat each other.

Before Getting Started
On chart paper use markers in three different colors to make three headings:
- What Does Grouchy Mean?
- What Makes You Angry?
- How Do You Calm Down?

Part One
1. Gather children in the library area during circle or meeting time. Show them the book and ask them what they think it is about. Does anyone know what it means to be *grouchy*?
2. Write down what children have to say under the "What Does Grouchy Mean?" heading on the chart paper.
3. Read the story. As the pages go on, children can participate in responsive reading, repeating the phrases that appear on each page: "You want to fight?" and "You're not big enough anyway." You might want to stop on certain pages to comment: "This ladybug isn't having a very happy day." "Does anyone have an idea why the ladybug might be feeling so grouchy?" Record their answers on the chart.

Part Two
1. Hold up *The Grouchy Ladybug* and briefly review the story. Review the "What Does Grouchy Mean?" list on the chart.
2. Ask children, "What makes you angry?" Write their responses on the chart paper. Have children talk about how they feel when they are angry (for example, upset, hot, wanting to punch something).

3. Follow up with a question about what children do to calm down when they feel angry, and write those answers underneath the "How Do You Calm Down?" section of the chart.

4. Review children's responses.

5. Ask, "Is there anything we can put in the 'Let's Calm Down' Corner that would help you when you are feeling grouchy or angry?" If at all possible, it is important to follow through on children's suggestions.

Note: As an alternative or addition to this activity, you may want to have children draw pictures and dictate a sentence about what makes them angry and what makes them feel better.

ACTIVITY

A Sad, Mad, Glad Chart

Setting
Circle time

Materials
- Chart paper divided into three columns with a face depicting sad, mad, or glad expressions at the top of each column

Time
15 min.

What Children Will Do
Talk about what makes them feel sad, mad, or glad

What Children Will Learn
How to recognize and name their feelings

1. Remind children about all the feelings they have been talking about. Explain that everyone has many feelings. Explain that today you have chosen three feelings to talk about: sad, mad, and glad. You may need to point out to children that *glad* is another word for *happy*.
2. Ask children if they notice anything about the words. Someone may recognize that the words rhyme. If not, point it out to them.
3. Before starting the chart, ask children to think about what it feels like when they are sad, when they are mad, and when they are glad.
4. Show children the chart you have prepared and point out the different expressions on the faces at the top of each column.
5. Begin with the sad column and ask children to take turns saying something that makes them feel sad. Put each child's name next to his or her words.
6. Continue the process with the mad column and the glad column.
7. Summarize the discussion. Point out similarities and differences in each column.

 SAD

Jocelyn–Being by myself
Alexandra–Mommy leaving
Daniel–Someone kicking me
Ciara–Someone taking my toy
Darius–When I get hurt/a booboo

 MAD

Daniel–When I get a time-out in my room
Miss Sharon–When my friends do not listen to me
Jocelyn–When I tease my sister and get a time-out
Jennifer–When my daddy takes my toys away

 GLAD

David–When the sun is out
Michael–When Mommy picks me up from school
Franklin–When Mommy brought me toys
Alvin–When Mommy gives me soda
Miss Millie–When I go to the movies

ACTIVITY

A Sad, Mad, Glad Poem

What Children Will Do	**What Children Will Learn**
Create a feelings poem and drawing	Repetition and rhyme Vocabulary Word play

Setting
Library area

Materials
- "Sad, Mad, Glad" chart (see previous activity on page 74)
- Poetry books
- Chart paper
- Colored markers (reflecting feelings, for example, blue for sad, red for mad, green for glad)
- Drawing paper
- Crayons

Time
Part One—10 min.
Part Two—10 min.
(per small group)
Part Three—15 min.

Young children love repetition and rhymes, and playing with words is an essential emerging literacy activity that is fun and skill building.

Part One

1. Bring out the "Sad, Mad, Glad" chart and review some of the things that the children expressed.
2. Ask children if they remember what we call words that sound alike except for the beginning letter. If no one remembers, tell children the word is *rhyme*.
3. Read children one or two poems that rhyme. Two good resources are *My Song Is Beautiful: Poems and Pictures in Many Voices* selected by Mary Ann Hoberman and *Dog Days: Rhymes Around the Year,* by Jack Prelutsky (see Annotated Bibliography for details). As you read, emphasize the rhyming words.

Part Two

1. Working in small groups, tell children that you were thinking they could make a "Sad, Mad, Glad" poem for the class library. Give them a sample opening line, for example, "Some things make me sad, or mad, or glad."
2. Ask if anyone can think of a line for the poem about being sad (I cry when I am sad). Follow by a line about feeling mad (I get red when I am mad), and then one about feeling glad (I smile when I am glad).
3. Write the poem on chart paper, using a different color marker to match the feeling expressed in each line.

Part Three

1. Have children make "Sad, Mad, Glad" drawings to illustrate the poem.
2. Mount the poem and drawings in a display on the wall or bulletin board.

ACTIVITY
Body Talk

Setting
Classroom or play yard

Materials
- Puppets

Time
15-20 min.

What Children Will Do
Explore body language

What Children Will Learn
Appropriate means of expression
Sense of self and effect on others
Strategies for helping

1. Bring children together in the classroom or yard. Introduce the idea of body talk: "Today we're going to work on a different way to talk about feelings. Usually we talk with words. We say, 'I feel sad. I feel angry. I feel happy.' Can anyone think of a way we can tell how we feel without using any words?"

2. If children don't come up with ideas, ask questions to prompt their thinking.

- If we're unhappy or frightened, what sound do we make? (You may need to give a clue by making a crying sound.)
- How about if we feel angry? How do we look?
- How do we look when we are sad?

Tell children that they just showed their feelings without using any words.

3. Explain that we can show feelings with our bodies, and when we do we are using "body language."

4. Use hand puppets to demonstrate different feelings without words and ask children to guess what feelings the puppets are showing.

5. Ask children if they can think of other feelings the puppets can show without words, for example, fear, hurt, and love.

Friendship Theme

Background

Children come into school knowing the word *friend,* but they do not fully understand the concepts that underlie the word. We also cannot assume that young children understand how to act with their friends. In fact, often they may not realize that some of their actions can make their friends feel sad, intimidated, or even frightened. They do know, however, that saying, "You're not my friend," is hurtful. The activities in this section will help children learn ways to be a friend and ways not to be a friend.

Friendship is comprised of many things, including the ability to "give and take," share, empathize, act kindly, and cooperate. Making new friends is an important part of preschool, and over the course of a school year, children will experience many aspects of friendship. Through stories, discussions, drawings, and brief puppet plays, you can help children form positive friendships and deepen their understanding of what friendship and friendly behavior means.

Concepts Learned in the Friendship Theme

- empathy
- sharing
- cooperation
- friendship

How to Be a Friend

Setting

Library or meeting area

Materials

- *How to Be a Friend: A Guide to Making Friends and Keeping Them* by Laurie Krasny Brown and Marc Brown
- Chart paper
- Markers

Time

Part One—15 min.
Part Two—15 min.

What Children Will Do

Listen to a story
Talk about their understanding of what it means to be a friend

What Children Will Learn

Vocabulary
Articulation
About concepts related to friendship

How to Be a Friend: A Guide to Making Friends and Keeping Them *is an excellent introduction to the topic of friendship.*

Part One

1. Hold up the cover of *How to Be a Friend.* Ask children what they think the book might be about. Point to the word *friend,* and see if anyone recognizes it or can tell you the beginning letter. Read the title of the book.

2. Read the first part of the story (through page 19), which focuses on making friends.

3. Pick out three or four aspects of the story you would like to discuss further. On a first reading, you may want to choose the simpler concepts. For example, asking someone to play (page 6), liking each other (pages 10-11), and sharing (page 12).
   Note: Read the story several times during the school year and discuss different aspects each time.

Part Two

1. On chart paper, write "Ways to Be a Friend." Explain to children that you want to talk about their ideas about being a friend. As needed, ask questions to prompt the discussion:

   - Does a friend have to be your age?
   - Does anyone have a grownup friend?
   - How do friends treat each other?
   - Do friends stand up for each other?

2. Write children's ideas on the "Ways to Be a Friend" chart. Hang the chart near the "Let's Work It Out" table, and review from time to time.
   Note: As an addition to the activity, take a picture of each child and a picture of the whole class together holding hands. Put the individual pictures around the "Ways to Be a Friend" chart and the class picture at the bottom of the chart.

Ways Not to Be a Friend

What Children Will Do
Recognize, discuss, and compare friendly/unfriendly behavior

What Children Will Learn
Vocabulary
Consequences of unfriendly behavior

Setting
Library or meeting area

Materials
- *How to Be a Friend: A Guide to Making Friends and Keeping Them* by Laurie Krasny Brown and Marc Brown
- "Ways to Be a Friend" chart
- Chart paper
- Markers
- Drawing materials

Time
20 min.

How to Be a Friend has a section on ways not to be a friend that is a good catalyst for a discussion about behavior that is not friendly.

1. Remind children about their previous discussion about friendship and review the chart they made with the children's pictures and the class picture as decoration.
2. Hold up *How to Be a Friend.* Tell children that today, you will be reading a different part of the book.
3. Open the book to page 20. Pass the book around so children can get a close look at the pictures. Ask if anyone has an idea about what the pictures show.
4. Tell children that this part of the book is called, "Ways Not to Be a Friend." Point out that the word, "Not," is in italics, and explain that this means it's very important.
5. Read pages 20-23. Discuss each picture as you read. For example:

   - How does it make you feel if someone calls you a bad name?
   - How would you feel if someone won't let you play?
   - Have you ever been teased? Did it make you feel bad or sad?
   - What if someone always wants to be the boss of every game? Is that fair?

6. List children's ideas about "Ways Not to Be a Friend" on a chart.
7. Hang the two charts side by side.
8. Ask children to think about the two charts so that they are ready to draw pictures about how to be a friend and ways not to be a friend.

ACTIVITY

Friendly/Unfriendly Pictures

Setting

Circle time and tables

Materials

- Drawing paper
- Crayons or markers
- "Ways to Be a Friend"/"Ways Not to Be a Friend" charts (from previous activities on pages 78 and 79)

Time

Part One–drawing activities over several days– 15 min. per activity; Part Two–15 min. per small group

What Children Will Do

Translate what they have been learning about friendship into drawings

Draw pictures that express ways to be friendly and unfriendly

Dictate sentences related to friendship

What Children Will Learn

Vocabulary

Fine-motor skills

Self-expression

Positive and negative aspects of friendship

Comparison

Part One

1. Read the "Ways to Be a Friend"/"Ways Not to be a Friend" charts to the children. Compare the charts. How are they different?

2. Ask children to draw two pictures, one about being a good friend and one about not being a good friend. If some children need help formulating their ideas, go back and review what they said on the charts.

3. As the children finish their drawings, ask them to tell you about the picture, and write a sentence to convey their ideas.
   Note: This activity can take place over several days. If you cannot get to every child during drawing time, you can put some pictures aside and add the sentences with the children later in the day.

Part Two

1. Working in small groups, ask each child to share the drawings she or he has made. Be sure to read the sentence that the child has dictated to go with the drawing.

2. Summarize the friendly and unfriendly things that children have depicted.

3. Make a two-part class book of the friendly/unfriendly drawings so you and the children can review them throughout the year (see page 53 for directions on how to make a book).

Puppet Friends

What Children Will Do	**What Children Will Learn**	**Setting**
Create brief role-plays about friendship	Vocabulary How to convey an idea	Dramatic play area

Setting
Dramatic play area

Materials
- Hand puppets
- Friendship scenarios

Time
15 min. per small group

As children act out very brief scenarios, they will gain further understanding of friendship situations. At first, you will need to give children very simple scenarios to act out, and demonstrate one or two for them. With practice, children will be able to make up their own scenarios in the dramatic play area or at circle time, using more than two puppets at a time.

1. Explain to children that they are going to use hand puppets to make up little plays about friendship, and that everyone will have a turn. Then, during work time, gather a small group of six to eight children in the dramatic play area.

   Note: This activity may take place over several days, or you may want to do the activity as a whole group.

2. Demonstrate one or two scenarios:

   Scenario 1
   - **Puppet 1:** "Do you want to play with me?"
     Puppet 2: "Okay, let's play." (The puppets pretend to play.)

   Scenario 2
   - **Puppet 1:** "Do you want to be my friend?"
     Puppet 2: "Yes. What should we play?"
     Puppet 1: "Want to make a block building?"
     Puppet 2: "Okay. Let's go." (The puppets pretend to walk over to the block area.)

3. Ask if anyone has an idea for a puppet play about being friends. If someone volunteers, ask her or him to tell the idea to the other children. Then ask the child to take one puppet, choose someone to take the other puppet, and act out the idea. If no one volunteers, you may have to give the children an idea, and ask two children to be the actors.

ACTIVITY

The First Day of School

Setting

Library area

Materials

- *Will I Have a Friend?* by Miriam Cohen

Time

20 min.

What Children Will Do

Listen to the story and discuss various feelings related to new situations, for example, entering preschool

What Children Will Learn

Listening skills

About facial expressions and body language

How to relate their own feelings to those of others

1. Ask children to close their eyes and remember how they felt on the first day of school.

   - Did anyone feel a little scared?
   - Did school feel like a strange place?
   - Did anyone feel excited?
   - Did anyone wonder if they would have friends?

2. Hold up the book cover and ask children what they think the book might be about. Is it about preschool children? Can someone point to the word *friend?*

3. Tell children the name of the book (you can point out that the title is in the form of a question, with a question mark for punctuation), and read the story.

4. After the story, review selected pages for facial expressions and body language. Say, "Let's see if we can tell how Jim is feeling."

   - On the page where his Dad is saying "goodbye"—Point to Jim and ask children how they think he is feeling. How can they tell?
   - On the next page—Ask children to notice where Jim is standing. Is he in the group?
   - On the page where Jim is holding his clay man—Ask, "Does Jim look happier?" "Why?"
   - On the page where Paul shows Jim his truck—Ask children about what is happening. "Is Jim making a friend? How does he look now?"

5. Ask children to compare how Jim felt at the beginning and at the end of his first day in preschool. Point out the different facial expressions and body language on the pages where he is walking to school with his Dad, and walking home at the end of the day.

New Friend Day

What Children Will Do

Connect with someone new to play with and create a "New Friends" class book

What Children Will Learn

How to expand their friendship group

How to recognize shapes

Setting

Play yard and classroom

Materials

- Circles, squares, rectangles, triangles and other shapes cut from colored construction paper

Time

20-30 min.

In this outdoor activity, each child is paired with a new friend to play with during outdoor time, and then each pair talks about what they did together.

Note: *This activity can also be done indoors in the block area.*

Before Getting Started

- Prepare two of each shape (or three [see note below]) in the same color.

   Note: If you are going to group three children together, you will need three of that shape.

- Think about how to pair children (or create threesomes) for maximum diversity, for example, girls with boys; a quiet child with an outgoing child; two children who avoid each other.

1. When children arrive in the play yard, ask everyone to sit in a circle (children can sit around the sandbox, on the ground, or on big blocks). Tell everyone that today is "new friend" day. Ask children what they think that means. Explain that each person is going to be paired up with someone he or she doesn't usually play with during outdoor playtime.

   Note: Depending on the number of children in your group, you may need to have some threesomes.

2. Hold up the colored shapes and ask children to guess what they are for. Be sure to show them that there are two (or three) of each shape. Give out each pair of shapes to the children that you have chosen to play together. Tell children they can play any game they choose as long as it is safe, follows play yard rules, and they play together. Tell children to remember their game, because they are going to talk about it at circle time the next day.

3. If some pairs have a hard time getting started, you might want to suggest a game, for example, building with the outdoor blocks, riding bicycles together, digging in the sandbox, or running races. Observe as the new friends play so you can help them learn to play together and get along, and then tell what happened when they have circle time the next day.

New Friend Book

Setting
Circle time and library area

Materials
- Large drawing paper
- Crayons or markers

Time
20 min.

What Children Will Do
Draw pictures for a class book

What Children Will Learn
Fine motor skills
Self-expression
Vocabulary
How to recognize shapes

This activity is a continuation of the previous activity, New Friend Day.

1. At circle time, remind children about their New Friend Day, and ask pairs of children to talk about the games they played together.
2. Write down the name of each pair of children and the game they played on a piece of large drawing paper. Paste the identifying pair of shapes on the top of each pair's page.
3. Ask each pair of children to draw a "new friend" picture to illustrate their page in the book.
   Note: If you think it will work better, draw a line to divide the page in half.
4. Bind the pictures into a "New Friends" book. If possible, laminate the pages so they will be sturdier.
5. Put the class book in the library. When children fall back into their regular play patterns read their book to them to remind them about the fun of making new friends.

What Does It Mean to Be Kind?

What Children Will Do
Create an "Acts of Kindness" chart for the classroom

What Children Will Learn
About the meaning of the words *kind* and *kindness*

About the importance of kindness in the classroom, school, and community

Setting
Meeting area, work tables or floor in the art area

Materials
- Chart paper
- Markers
- Colored paper
- Poster board (approximately 20" x 30")
- Glue sticks
- Decorative art supplies–glitter, doilies, sequins, and so on

Time
Part One–10 min.
Part Two–ongoing a week or more
Part Three–20 min.

Because being kind to each other is such a key concept in creating a teasing and bullying-free classroom, it is worth taking time to clarify the meaning of the word "kind" and the concept of kindness.

Part One

1. Ask the children to close their eyes and listen to a story with no pictures. Tell them that they can imagine the pictures in their heads.

   Once there was a preschool class with 18 boys and girls. All the children had come to school together on the first day, which was many months ago. At first the children felt strange in their new school, but now they all knew each other and were friends. One day, at class meeting time their teacher said, "Children, tomorrow a new girl and boy will be joining our class. They are cousins and they come from a country where they speak a different language than English. The children's names are Elena and Jamil. I would like us to think about kind things we can do to make Elena and Jamil feel welcome in our class."

2. Say, "Let's pretend that we are that class. What kind things can we do to make Elena and Jamil feel welcome?"

3. Write the children's ideas on chart paper. If needed, prompt the discussion with questions:

   - Should we sing the "Hearty Welcome" song?
   - Should we share our favorite toys?
   - Should we ask them to play?

4. Explain that all the ideas can be called "acts of kindness" because they will make the new children feel welcome in the classroom.

Part Two

1. Tell children that you were thinking about the "acts of kindness" list they made after the Elena and Jamil story. Tell them you would like to make an "Acts of Kindness" poster for the classroom that will tell about the kind things children do for each other.

2. Ask children to tell you when someone does a kind thing for them, or when they do a kind thing for a classmate. Say that you will write them down.

3. At class meeting times be sure to ask if anyone has an "act of kindness" to tell about.

4. Continue to collect "acts of kindness" stories until each child has contributed and there are enough "acts" to fill a piece of poster board or bulletin board.

Part Three

1. Print the children's "acts of kindness" on small pieces of colored paper (or type them in large type on a computer). Be sure to attach each child's name to each act of kindness. Assemble the art supplies.

2. Print "Acts of Kindness" and the date on the top of the poster board.

3. Assemble children around tables or on the floor in the art area. Show the children the poster board and the printed stories.

4. Give out the stories and art supplies. Let children glue their stories on the poster board and draw a picture about their stories.
   Note: If the class is large, create two posters or let half the class work at one time.

5. Mount the poster in the classroom. Be sure to read the poster aloud.

6. Change the "acts of kindness" stories or create additional posters periodically.

CHAPTER 7

Teasing and Bullying Theme

Background

The difference between teasing and bullying is often a matter of degree. Make no mistake, both behaviors are harmful to the recipient and the perpetrator, but when a child is bullied, the consequences can be lifelong physical or psychological damage.

The generally accepted definition of bullying is a hurtful action carried out repeatedly over time. However, even isolated incidents of bullying can be extremely harmful, for example, beating someone up or disparaging a child's family. The general perception is that bullying is more physical than verbal, but mean words shouted in a young child's face or posted in a bathroom or on the Internet in the upper grades can be every bit as damaging.

Bullying often has a menacing quality to it and can create fear and despair for the recipient. It has been well documented that children who are bullied can develop physical symptoms such as headaches or stomachaches and often don't want to go to school. In extreme cases, bullying has led to childhood suicide (Portner, 2001). Bullying is an issue throughout the world, and adults are becoming aware that it must be addressed at every level of education. As preschool educators, we have an opportunity to prevent this behavior from becoming a part of our classroom environment.

It is important to help children develop problem-solving strategies to deal with teasing or bullying situations. Because the solutions children come up with need to be safe and developmentally appropriate, teachers must guide them away from using "superhero" tactics to solve problems. One good way is to base discussions and role-playing on situations that typically arise in preschool classrooms.

Part of what children need to know in teasing or bullying situations is when to seek adult help, which requires helping them understand the difference between tattling and telling. Even at preschool age, children know that tattling is unacceptable behavior, and a tattletale is usually an unpopular child. One of the activities in this section will help children distinguish between tattling (getting a child in trouble) and telling (helping a child who is being hurt physically or emotionally).

Children also need to understand that words can be as hurtful as a punch, and sometimes even more so. What we say affects the way we make another person feel. And standing by and watching or laughing when someone is being teased or bullied magnifies the hurt of the situation. The child being teased is humiliated, and the bystanders feel guilty, embarrassed, and powerless even though they might be laughing outwardly. Deep down they know it isn't funny, and they also know it could happen to them.

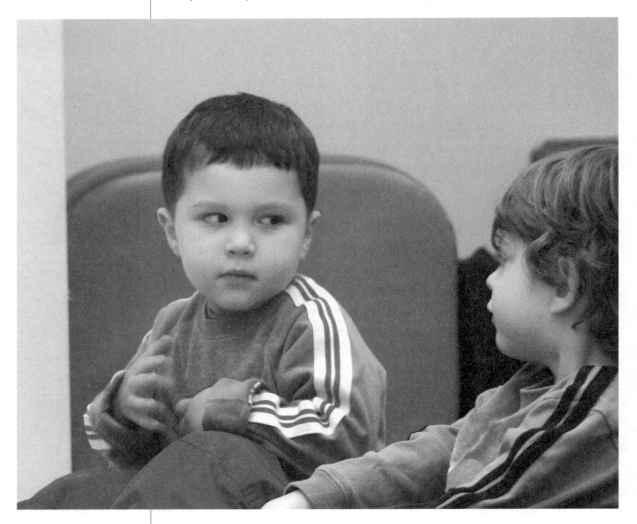

When laughter is an expression of fun, happiness, or humor it is a positive human emotion. However, when laughter is directed toward someone's appearance or as the result of a joke made at someone's expense, it can become hurtful and cruel. Activities will help children understand the difference between laughing at something that is funny, and laughing at (or making fun of) someone to create "bystander" laughter.

Many things can make children vulnerable to teasing and bullying: the foods they eat, their names, how they look, even their toys. By the time they enter preschool, three- and four-year-old children start to differentiate between "boy" toys and "girl" toys. Children pick up verbal and nonverbal messages from family members, friends, TV programming and commercials, and visits to the toy store, where packaging and color-coding gives a very strong, stereotyped sex-role message.

Teasing and bullying occur when a child is perceived as different, because, in many cases, other children are unfamiliar with that difference. This is why it is so important to read stories, have discussions, and role-play with puppets to talk about these issues and to help children become familiar and comfortable with differences.

Reference

Portner, J. 2001. *One in thirteen: The silent epidemic of teen suicide.* Beltsville, MD: Robins Lane Press.

Concepts Learned in the Teasing and Bullying Theme

- feelings (positive and negative)
- respect for self and others
- telling vs. tattling
- respect for space
- similarities and differences
- alike and different
- empathy

What Is Teasing?

Setting
Circle time

Materials
- Chart paper
- Markers

Time
10 min.

What Children Will Do
Discuss the meaning of the word *teasing*

What Children Will Learn
Vocabulary
About the word *definition* (describes what a word means)

1. Write the word, "teasing," at the top of the chart paper. Then ask children if they can explain what teasing is. Write their ideas, in their words, on the chart paper. Be sure to write each child's name next to his or her idea, for example, "Kaitlin thinks that teasing is calling someone names;" "Danny thinks teasing is when you laugh at someone's clothes;" "Nina thinks teasing is when you make fun of the way someone talks."

2. When all children have had a chance to contribute, use their words to create a definition. The definition can have several parts. For example: Teasing is calling someone names or making fun of them. Teasing is a way to hurt someone using words.

3. Explain to children that what they have done is create a definition, which is a way to explain what a word means.

Note: To go along with this activity, create a "We Like Each Other" poster. Children can dictate something they like about another child and draw a picture to illustrate their compliment. Mount the poster at children's eye level. Be sure that every child in the class is represented on the poster.

ACTIVITY
What Is Bullying?

What Children Will Do	**What Children Will Learn**	**Setting**
Create definitions of a bully	Vocabulary What it means to be bullied	Circle time

Setting
Circle time

Materials
- Chart paper
- Markers
- Children's definitions of teasing (see previous activity on page 90)

Time
10 min.

1. At circle time, briefly review the chart with definition of the word *teasing*. Tell children that today they are going to create a definition for the word *bully*.

2. Write, "What does a bully do?" at the top of the chart paper. Then ask children to say what they think a bully is, for example, someone who punches to hurt someone. Write their ideas on the chart paper, using their words and writing each child's name next to her or his idea.

3. Remind children that a definition is a way to explain what a word means.

4. Once all children have had a chance to contribute to the "What does a bully do?" chart, use their words to create a definition of bullying.

    Note: Another way to help children understand about positive behavior is to create a "Freeze Game" that can be played indoors or outdoors. Ask children to sit in a circle on the floor, and explain the game. Tell children that they can run around until you say "Freeze!" Then everyone has to stop in place, listen to what you say, and think of an answer. Give an example; say, "A bully grabs toys away from other children, but it is better to _____." When children respond with something pro-social, such as "Ask for a turn," everyone is "unfrozen" and can run again.

ACTIVITY
What Should We Do?

Setting
Circle time or class meeting time

Materials
- Sets of three cutout stick figures for each child representing "walk away," "stand up for yourself," and "get help"
- Craft sticks (or cardboard strips)
- Scenarios (see activity)
- Children's definitions of teasing and a bully

Time
Part One—20 min.
Part Two 15—min.

What Children Will Do
Practice problem solving

What Children Will Learn
Safe and practical strategies for addressing teasing and bullying situations
How to use good judgment

The scenarios listed below are based on situations that typically arise in preschool classrooms. Use them as a guideline, but feel free to create scenarios that address situations specific to your classroom.

Before Getting Started
Cut out stick figure sets for each child and mount them on craft sticks.

Part One
1. During class meeting time, review children's definitions of teasing and bullying (see pages 90 and 91). Tell children that you want them to think of ways to solve some teasing and bullying problems. Ask if someone could explain the meaning of the word *problem*.
2. When you are sure children understand what a problem is, show them a sample of the stick figures, and talk about the solution each one represents. Give a set of the stick figures to each child. Say that you will tell them a little story, and then each person can pick the stick figure that he or she thinks would work best, and talk about ideas to help solve the problem. Demonstrate.

    Scenario: Maria and Danny pretend to be monsters. They always creep up behind Shelley and make very loud "monster" noises, which frighten her. It happens every day and Shelley is upset. What should she do?

3. Show the children the stick figure(s) that might work. For example, hold up the "stand up for yourself" figure and have Shelley say, "Go away, I don't like it when you yell at me." Ask children what to do if that doesn't work. Hold up the "get help" figure.

walk away

get help

stand up for yourself

Part Two

1. Choose one or two of the following scenarios with children (or make up your own versions).
   Note: The scenarios can be done as a whole group or with small groups of children in the dramatic play area.

   Scenario 1: Sometimes Mikey likes to play dress up with jewelry and skirts. Other children tell him, "That's for girls. Boys don't do that." And they laugh and tease him. What should Mikey do?

   As children discuss the scenario, ask questions to challenge their assumptions:

   - Don't we all like to pretend?
   - Is it okay for girls to dress up in men's hats and ties? Why? Why not?

   Scenario 2: Jessica and Phil are both four years old, and they are in the same class. Every day, Jessica calls Phil a baby and says he's too little to be in school. Phil gets very upset when Jessica says, "You're a baby," and some of the other children laugh. What should Phil do?

   Talk about the different solutions children chose, for example, "Sarah thinks Phil should stand up for himself, but Jake thinks he should just walk away and tell Jessica it doesn't bother him. How many children think both ideas might work. Also, was it right for some children to laugh? What could they have done instead?"

   Scenario 3: Stevie and Paul are in the same class. Every day, when the teacher isn't looking, Stevie punches Paul in the arm. Some of his classmates watch what is happening. Even though Paul has fun at school the rest of the time, he is scared of Stevie and wants to stay home instead. What should Paul do?

   Talk about the different solutions children choose, for example, "Mary thinks Paul should stand up for himself, but Eddie thinks he should get help from the teacher." Should Paul try to stand up to Stevie before he gets help from the teacher? Did any of Paul's classmates see what Stevie was doing? What could Paul's classmates have done to help? What would you do?

2. Sum up the lesson by reviewing the three strategies. Hold up each figure as you talk. Tell children that you will put the figures near the "Let's Work It Out" table to remind them of ways to solve problems.

ACTIVITY
Can Words Hurt Us?

What Children Will Do
Explore how everyday words such as animal names, used in certain ways, can be hurtful

What Children Will Learn
About the effect of their words on others
How common words can be used to hurt others

Setting
Circle time or meeting time

Materials
- Two hand puppets
- Pictures of a shrimp and a rat

Time
15 min.

1. Ask the question, "Do you ever think that words can hurt us?" Say, "Let's think about it." Give children a chance to talk about how words can be hurtful.

2. Explain to children that sometimes it is not the word itself, but the way it is used that makes them hurtful. Use the word *shrimp* as an example. Ask, "Does anyone know what a shrimp is?" Children may or may not know that a shrimp is a small sea creature. Show them a picture of a shrimp. Then say, "Let's watch the puppets to see how *shrimp* can become a hurtful word."

   Puppet 1: "You're too little to be in this class. You're a shrimp."
   Puppet 2: "I'm not a shrimp. I'm a person."
   Puppet 1: "You're a shrimp. Your name is 'Shrimpy.' Ha, ha."
   Puppet 2: "I don't want to be a shrimp. A shrimp is a little fish. I'm a boy."

   Show the puppet "Shrimpy," hanging its head and looking sad.

3. Talk about the puppet story with the children. How did being called "shrimp," make the puppet feel? Was "shrimp" a hurtful word?

4. Say, "Let's think about another word." Ask, "Does anyone know what a rat is?" Children will probably be able to describe a rat. If not, you can describe its physical characteristics and show a picture. "Let's watch the puppets to see how *rat* can become a hurtful word."

Puppet 1: "Give me that truck. I need it for my building."
Puppet 2: "I had it first, and I need it for my game. I'll give you a turn later."
Puppet 1: "I want it right now. Give it to me."
Puppet 2: "No, I won't. It's my turn."
Puppet 1: "You're a rat. Ratty, ratty, rat."
Puppet 2: "I'm not a rat. I was trying to be fair."

Show the puppet, "Rat," walking away and looking sad.

5. Talk about the puppet story with the children. How did being called "rat," make the puppet feel? Was rat a hurtful word?
6. Summarize the discussion. "We really need to think about not using words in a way that can hurt another person's feelings. Think about how we might feel if someone called us an animal name just to make us feel bad."
7. Close by saying that animals are fine creatures in nature, but calling people by animal names hurts their feelings.

Making Puppets

What Children Will Do
Create paper bag puppets

What Children Will Learn
Creativity

Small motor skills

About the parts of a face

Setting
Art area

Materials
- Small brown lunch bags
- Shredded newspaper for stuffing
- Craft sticks
- Rubber bands
- Crayons
- Glue sticks
- Yarn for hair (optional)
- Large box or basket

Time
30 min.

1. Assemble the materials and show them to children when they are gathered in the art area. Explain that each child will be making a puppet to use in a little play about teasing. **Note:** You may want to make the puppets with small groups of children instead of the whole class. Children will need adult assistance to secure the craft stick and the bottom of the bag with a rubber band.

2. Have each child draw a face on the front of her or his bag with the crayons. You may want to review the parts of the face—a pair of eyes, a nose, a mouth, a pair of ears (remind children that "pair" is another word for two).

   Note: Because you will need two puppets for your part in the play, you may want to make your puppets as the children make theirs.

3. Show the children how to stuff shredded newspaper into their bags and insert a craft stick into the bottom as a holder.

draw a face!

stuff with newspaper

insert craft stick

decorate!

Juan

4. Help each child wrap a rubber band tightly around the bottom of the bag and the stick. Then write the child's name on the craft stick.
5. Encourage the children to draw hair or glue wool "hair" on the puppet.
6. Put the puppets in a large box or basket.

ACTIVITY
It Isn't Funny!

What Children Will Do

Participate in a puppet play

Explore the meaning of the word *bystander*

What Children Will Learn

Creativity

Role-playing skills

About being a bystander (that it is not acceptable behavior)

Vocabulary

Setting

Dramatic play area

Materials

- Children's homemade puppets (see previous activity on page 97)
- Scenarios from the "What Should We Do?" activity (see pages 92-94)
- 2 teacher-made or purchased puppets

Time

20 min.

1. Gather children in the dramatic play area. Remind them about the "What Should We Do?" activity (see pages 92-94). Ask if anyone remembers the problem about children laughing when Jason teased Phil and called him a baby.

   Jessica and Phil are both four years old, and they are in the same class. Every day, Jessica calls Phil a baby and says he's too little to be in school. Phil gets very upset when Jessica says, "You're a baby," and some of the other children laugh. What should Phil do?

   Tell children that when you watch someone being teased, it is called being a bystander.

2. Explain that the paper bag puppets are going to act out being bystanders, while your puppets act out the Jessica and Phil teasing story. Ask three children to come forward with their puppets. Help the children decide how they will act as bystanders, for example, do nothing, laugh, or say, "baby." You may have to cue children until they understand role-playing.

3. Next, choose three other children to use their puppets as bystanders while you act out another teasing scenario. Again, let children decide the action their puppets will take.

4. After the role-plays, ask children to think about how it feels to be a bystander. How would they feel if someone was watching while they were being teased? Would it be a good feeling? Would it feel hurtful? Why?

5. Help children understand that being a bystander is not acceptable. Talk about what they could do if they see someone being teased:

   - Tell the person to stop the teasing.
   - Ask an adult to help.

6. Teach children that they never should join in the teasing.

Everyone Likes Special Foods

Setting

Library area

Materials

- *Yoko* by Rosemary Wells
- Chart paper
- Markers or crayons
- Half sheets of drawing paper

Time

Part One—15 min.
Part Two—20 min.

What Children Will Do

Listen and discuss *Yoko*

What Children Will Learn

Respect for others
Vocabulary
Descriptive language

Many young children are quite particular about the foods they eat. How food looks and smells can seem enticing or quite the opposite, and it can make some children vulnerable to teasing. Usually, the teasing is based on unfamiliarity with foods from different cultures. In Yoko, *the teacher uses "International Day" to introduce children to foods from various cultures.*

Part One

1. Read the story about Yoko.
2. Discuss the story. Ask:

   - Why did the children make fun of Yoko's lunch?
   - What could the children have done instead?
   - Were the children teasing Yoko?
   - How did Timothy and Yoko become friends?

Part Two

1. Briefly review the main points of the story.
2. Ask children to talk about how they would feel if someone made fun of their lunch. Would they feel welcome or unwelcome? Sad? Angry? Hurt?
3. Ask children if there is a special kind of food that their family eats. Do they eat it every day? On special holidays? List children's special foods on chart paper.
4. Ask children to draw a picture of their "special foods" and decorate the chart with them.

Everyone's Name Is Special

What Children Will Do

Listen and discuss a story about
  making fun of someone's name
Talk about children's own names

What Children Will Learn

Respect for others
Vocabulary
Empathy

Setting

Library area

Materials

- *Chrysanthemum*
  by Kevin Henkes

Time

Part One—20 min.
Part Two—10 min.

The story of Chrysanthemum *is an example of how hurtful teasing (in this case making fun of a name) can be, and how it can harm a child's sense of self.*

Part One

1. Introduce the book, *Chrysanthemum*. Ask if anyone knows what a chrysanthemum is. Point to the word and the mouse (girl) on the cover, and see if children can figure out that Chrysanthemum is a name.
2. Read the story. On the teasing pages, call attention to the way the mice children's remarks are making Chrysanthemum feel. Observe her body language as well as her words. On the pages that show her at home, call attention to the way Chrysanthemum's parents support and comfort her.

Part Two

1. Remind children about the story.
2. Ask children to think about how special their name feels to them, and how they would feel if someone made fun of it.
3. Ask children to raise their hands if they know how they got their name. Ask some questions to spark their thinking:

   - Were you named after a special person? Who was that?
   - Did your parents pick a name because they liked the way it sounded?
   - Were you named for a special place or a special country?
   - Does anyone else in your family have the same name?

4. Ask children if they would like to add a rule about not making fun of people's names to the class rules.

ACTIVITY
New and Different Is Okay

Setting
Library area

Materials
- *The Brand New Kid* by Katie Couric
- "I Feel Welcome" and "I Feel Unwelcome" charts (from previous activities, see pages 61-66)
- Construction paper
- Markers

Time
Part One—20 min.
Part Two—15 min.

What Children Will Do
Read and discuss a story about what it feels like to be new in school; recall how they felt; revisit the "I Feel Welcome"/"I Feel Unwelcome" charts

What Children Will Learn
Empathy
Relationship of self to others

The Brand New Kid *is about how children learn to accept someone who is different.*

Part One
1. Introduce the story. Tell children it is about a little boy who felt some of the same things they felt when they were new at school.
2. Read the story. Point out Lazlo's facial expressions as you read. Ask, "Does Lazlo look happy? Does he look upset?" "Unhappy?"
3. On the page showing the lunchroom, point out that Lazlo is sitting all by himself and that a boy is teasing him by shooting a straw paper at him. Ask the children why they think the boy is teasing Lazlo.

Part Two
1. Hold up *The Brand New Kid.* Tell children you would like them to talk more about the story.
2. Draw children's attention to the page where Lazlo's mother is shown with tears in her eyes. Ask children to think about how their mothers or fathers might feel if their child was so unhappy in school? Can unhappiness spread?

3. Talk about what made Lazlo feel more comfortable in school. Was it very hard for Ellie to be a friend? Did it make her happy?

4. Ask children to think about how they felt at the beginning of school. Write down children's remarks. If they don't remember, ask a few questions:

   - Did anyone feel a little scared?
   - Did school seem strange to you?
   - Did you wonder about making friends?

5. Re-read the" I Feel Welcome" and "I Feel Unwelcome" charts.

6. Give out markers and sheets of construction paper folded in half. Ask the children to make a "Welcome" card for Lazlo. They can draw a picture or a design and they can write or dictate their name and some words of welcome, for example, "Hello, Lazlo" or "Welcome."

I FEEL WELCOME...

When people share their show and tell
_____

When I color with my friends
_____

When I play cars
_____

When my friend reads me a book
_____

When my friends are near me on their mats
_____

When I am asked to be a helper

Teasing Hurts

Setting
Library area

Materials
- *Flop-Ear* by Guido Van Genechten

Time
Part One—10 min.
Part Two—15 min.

What Children Will Do
Read and discuss the story of Flop-Ear with a focus on the pages depicting teasing

What Children Will Learn
How hurtful teasing can be
About accepting differences

In this story, Flop-Ear (a rabbit) is teased because his ears are different. He tries to be like everyone else and comes to understand that everyone is different.

Part One
1. Read the story. Ask children to think about Flop-Ear's feelings while you are reading.
2. Talk briefly about what the other rabbits do to hurt Flop-Ear's feelings.

Part Two
1. Tell children that you have been thinking about all the ways that the other rabbits teased Flop-Ear.
2. Go through the pages looking at the pictures but not reading the text. Talk about the teasing and how it is making Flop-Ear feel.

- On the second page, the rabbits are taunting Flop-Ear and he is crying. Ask children, "What have the rabbits done to make Flop-Ear feel hurt and sad?" Help children realize that calling names, pointing and laughing are forms of teasing. They are not the way to treat a friend or anyone. Ask, "How do you know that Flop-Ear is sad?"
- On the page where Flop-Ear is wearing a hat to hide his ears, talk about the mean expression on the other rabbit's faces. They are jeering at Flop-Ear. Again, ask children if that is the way to treat anyone. How would that kind of laughing make them feel?
- On the page where Flop-Ear has tied a balloon to his ear, point out that, again, the rabbits are laughing *at* Flop-Ear, not *with* him.
- Read and discuss the pages where Flop-Ear thinks about cutting off his ear, and how sad being teased about his difference makes him feel. Help children notice the body language in the drawings. Point out that the tree is leaning just like Flop-Ear's ear.

- Use the final page (where the rabbits all put carrots on their ears) to talk about how being different is part of what makes people interesting to each other.

3. Summarize the discussion and make the following key points:

- Teasing can make someone feel very sad.
- Friends don't hurt each other.
- It is okay to be different.

Toys for Boys and Girls

Setting
Library area

Materials
- *William's Doll* by Charlotte Zolotow

Time
Part One—20 min.
Part Two—10 min.

What Children Will Do
Listen to *William's Doll* and discuss toy stereotyping

What Children Will Learn
New ways to think about toys
Concepts of fairness
Sensitivity to name calling

William's Doll *is a classic story that addresses the issue of "girl" toys and "boy" toys.*

Note: *You are probably aware of the toys and games that children in your class regularly select. If not, make notes for a week about typical choices that the girls and boys make before reading the story.*

Part One
1. Read the story. Ask some questions to spark a discussion:

   - Why did William want a doll?
   - Ask the boys, "Did you ever want a doll? Does anyone have a doll of his own?"
   - Ask the girls, "Did you ever want something that was called a boy's toy?"
   - Why did his brother and his brother's friend call William names? Was that a nice thing to do? How do you think William felt when he was called names?
   - Did William's father want him to have a doll? How do you know?
   - Did William's Grandma want him to have a doll? Why?

Part Two
1. Briefly review *William's Doll*.
2. Here are some questions to start the discussion:

   - Is it fair that some toys are for boys and some are for girls?
   - Ask the boys, "Did anyone ever make fun of you for wanting a toy that is usually for girls?"
   - Ask the girls, "Did anyone ever make fun of you for wanting a toy that is usually for boys?"
   - Can we change that idea in our class, so both boys and girls can choose any toy they like?

3. If children are not ready to accept that boys and girls can play with any toy that interests them, ask them to think about it. Perhaps you can talk about some toys in the classroom that both girls and boys enjoy, such as clay, playdough, blocks, puzzles, Legos™, and dress-up clothes.

4. At another time, read *William's Doll* and continue the discussion.

Telling or Tattling

Setting

Meeting or dramatic play area

Materials

- 2 hand puppets
- Chart paper
- Markers

Time

Part One—15 min.

Part Two—15 min.

Part Three (optional)

What Children Will Do

Learn the difference between tattling and telling

Respond to short puppet scenarios depicting tattling or telling situations

What Children Will Learn

How to understand the important difference between tattling on someone or telling when someone needs adult help

Part One

1. Ask if anyone can explain the meaning of the word *tattle*. After children have expressed their views, summarize:

    - Tattling is trying to get someone in trouble.
    - Tattling is trying to get a grownup's attention when no one or nothing is being hurt.

2. Ask children, "When do you think it's okay to tell on someone?" If children don't know, prompt them. "What if you saw one child hurt another? Would that be a good reason to tell an adult?" Give children reasons for telling:

    - Telling is okay if one child is hurting another child on purpose.
    - Telling is okay when you or a friend needs protection or is feeling scared.

3. Write "Tattling" on one half of a piece of chart paper and "Telling" on the other. Summarize what each word means.

Part Two

1. Introduce the children to the two puppets. It doesn't matter if they represent two boys or two girls. Give the puppets names, but don't use any that are actual names of children in class.

2. Tell the children that you are going to act out some scenes with the puppets, and their job will be to decide if it's a tattling or telling situation.

    Scene 1: Puppet Joe sees Puppet Zack take an extra cookie from the snack tray. Puppet Joe runs to tell the teacher.

Is Joe tattling or telling? If children don't think puppet Joe is tattling, remind them that tattling is trying to get someone in trouble.

3. Offer another puppet scene, this time about telling.

   Puppet Bill sees a bigger child punching his friend Puppet Mike on the playground, and he runs to tell the school aide about it.

   Ask, "Is puppet Bill telling or tattling?" Again, remind children that telling is okay when someone is being hurt.

Part Three

1. Use the puppet scenes below on another day soon after the first lesson, or when tattling versus telling situations arise.

Puppet Tattling Scenes

- Puppet Shana and puppet Tina want the same toy at the same time. Tina gets angry and runs to tell the teacher that Shana won't share.
- Puppet Jason tells the teacher that puppet Aaron tore a page in a book while he was reading it.

Puppet Telling Scenes

- Puppet Grace sees Puppet Meeka push someone off the slide and runs to tell the teacher about it.
- Puppet Stevie feels afraid that Puppet Jarod is going to hit him again like he did yesterday when no one was looking.

Note: Feel free to make up your own puppet scenarios based on incidents you have observed. Be sure to give the puppets names that are different from those of children in the class.

Annotated Bibliography

Picture books are one of the major resources for addressing teasing and bullying behavior at the preschool level. Fortunately, there is a wealth of good children's literature that can be used to support the main themes of community, feelings, friendship, and teasing and bullying. Developmentally appropriate picture books provide a non-threatening way to help children develop empathy toward others; build understanding and appreciation of differences; and explore a broad range of feelings. And, in addition to developing social skills, picture books are the tools of emerging literacy. Through daily reading children learn to listen, to discuss themes and ideas, learn vocabulary, and develop aesthetic appreciation for different art styles, colors, and graphic design. In short, there is a wealth of learning to be gained from children's literature.

The books for this bibliography have been selected because they address the themes of this curriculum and because they contribute to a caring learning environment for all children. They depict children and families from diverse cultural and racial groups; they avoid showing girls and boys in stereotyped roles; and they are examples of high-quality literature in terms of language and illustration. These books teach in myriad ways.

All the books have been chosen for a preschool age group. Those especially appropriate for three-year-olds are marked 3*. Every effort has been made to choose books that are currently in print and easily available through bookstores or online. Some excellent books are out of print but can be found in libraries. Each title is annotated, but we suggest that you read the books before you present them to children. Remember, good picture books are published every year, so always be on the lookout for new selections that can be added to your collection. Please share this bibliography with the parents in your school, and ask them to join you in finding new resources.

The bibliography also includes a selection of books and websites for adults. Included are authors that have a developmentally appropriate approach to issues of teasing and bullying. The websites are useful for current information and resources.

Enjoy reading with children!

Books for Children

Agassi, Martine
Illustrations by Marieka Heinlen
Hands Are Not for Hitting
Minneapolis, MN: Free Spirit Publishing (2000)
A book about all the wonderful creative and practical things children can do with their hands, with some pages devoted to reasons why hands are not for hitting. Clear illustrations and bright colors add to the fun of reading the story. Note: There is a Board Book version with fewer pages for children 18 months to 3 years of age.

Aliki
Feelings
New York: Mulberry Books (imprint of William Morrow & Co.) (1984)
A Reading Rainbow Book.
Aliki illustrates a broad range of very real emotions felt by children. The illustrations are small, amusing and whimsical. It can be read selectively, and since many of the pictures are small and very detailed, it will work best if read one-on-one or to a small group of children rather than as a class story. For three-year-olds select a few pages at a time, for example, pages 8-9; page 19.

Brown, Laura Krasny and Brown, Marc
How to Be a Friend: A Guide to Making Friends and Keeping Them
Boston: Little, Brown and Company (1998)
Dinosaurs representing children look at friendship from many aspects—feelings, sharing, helping each other, fairness. The second part of the book deals with "Ways Not to Be a Friend"—excluding, bossing, teasing, bullying, and fighting.

Carle, Eric
The Grouchy Ladybug
New York: Harper Collins Publishers (new edition, 1996)
A very grouchy ladybug who doesn't like to share offers to fight with a friendly ladybug over a breakfast of aphids. She goes on to challenge all kinds of bigger creatures, but flies away when they accept her offer to fight. After 12 hours of being grouchy and looking for a fight, the grouchy ladybug is ready to share a dinner of aphids with the friendly ladybug. An excellent resource for discussing bullying and how to give up that behavior.

The Cheltenham Elementary School Kindergartners
Photographs by Laura Dwight
We Are All Alike: We Are All Different
New York: Scholastic (2002)
Celebrating diversity, children's drawings and photographs reinforce multicultural and bias-free learning as it really happens at the Cheltenham School.

Cohen, Miriam
Pictures by Lillian Hoban
Will I Have a Friend?
New York: Simon & Schuster Books for Young Readers (1967)
A classic story about children's concerns at the beginning of preschool. How will I fit in? Will I make a friend? And, how comforting it is when everything works out.

Couric, Katie
Illustrated by Marjorie Priceman
The Brand New Kid
New York: Doubleday (2000)
New, foreign, different-looking Lazlo has to endure teasing and exclusion in his new school, until one girl decides to befriend him and helps others see him as a friend not a stranger. Interesting illustrations show a lot about body language. Best for four-year-olds.

Fox, Mem
Illustrated by Leslie Staub
Whoever You Are
San Diego: Voyager Books (Harcourt, Inc., 2001)
A Reading Rainbow Book
A global perspective on alike and different. Beautiful, magical pictures add to the feelings that the world is a wonderful place full of human diversity. 3*

Frame, Jeron Ashford
Illustrated by R. Gregory Christie
Yesterday I Had the Blues
Berkeley, CA: Tricycle Press (2003)
An African-American boy describes all the feelings he and his family experience. Moods are described by color—blue is feeling low and sad, red is angry, green is feeling good and optimistic—and words are used poetically. The story, however, is about everyday activities that children will understand.

Gainer, Cindy
I'm Like You, You're Like Me: A Child's Book About Understanding and Celebrating Each Other
Minneapolis, MN: Free Spirit Publishing, Inc. (1998)
Multicultural illustrations depict the many things children have in common, and the ways that they are different. Diverse family structures, manners, sharing, and kindness are all addressed in language that is calming and comforting for young children. 3*

Harris, Robie, H.
Illustrated by Jan Ormerod
I Am Not Going to School Today!
New York: Margaret K. McElderry Books (2003)
An excellent expression of the fears a child might feel before going to school for the first time, and how a caring preschool setting helps to create a sense of comfort and belonging.

Hammerseng, Kathryn, M.
Illustrated by Dave Garbot
Telling Isn't Tattling
Seattle, WA: Parenting Press, Inc. (1995)

A very useful book of brief stories that help children understand the difference between tattling and telling. Some scenarios are about play situations between children, and others about potential abuse involving adults.

Henkes, Kevin
Chrysanthemum
New York: Greenwillow Books (1991)
Chrysanthemum is a self-confident little girl (mouse) who loves being named for a flower, until she goes to school for the first time and is teased about her name. The story is an example of how hurtful teasing can be, and how it can harm a child's sense of self. Fortunately, there is a happy ending, in the person of a beloved music teacher, whose first name is Delphinium.

Hoberman, Mary Ann (selected by)
My Song Is Beautiful: Poems and Pictures in Many Voices
Boston: Little Brown and Company (1994)
A beautiful book for introducing children to poetry. The collection includes poems by Langston Hughes, A.A. Milne, Ruth Krauss and Nikki Giovanni. The poem "ME I AM" by the children's poet, Jack Prelutsky, is a celebration of each child's individuality. 3*

Jahn-Clough, Lisa
My Friend and I
Boston: Houghton Mifflin Company (1999)
A story that conveys how a boy and a girl become friends, have great fun playing together, fight over a toy bunny they can't share, feel miserable without each other, and learn to forgive and make up.

Krauss, Jack
Pictures by Jose Areugo
Leo the Late Bloomer
New York: Windmill Books (1971)
This story of a young tiger, whose development is a little slower than expected, helps children and adults understand that sometimes all that is needed is a little more time. 3*

Lalli, Judy

Photographs by Douglas L. Mason-Fry

I Like Being Me: Poems for Children About Feeling Special, Appreciating Others, and Getting Along

Minneapolis, MN: Free Spirit Publishing (1997)

Simple rhyming poems explore issues important to the everyday lives of young children. Themes include being kind, solving problems, dealing with feelings, being a friend, and more. A leader's guide is also available.

Lionni, Leo

It's Mine!

New York: Alfred A. Knopf (1985)

Three quarrelsome young frogs who are always shouting, "It's mine," have to learn to share and cooperate to save themselves when a big storm comes along. The story helps young children see that sharing and cooperation are important in school and in the world. 3*

Lionni, Leo

Swimmy

New York: Pantheon (1968)

A classic book by the beloved children's author teaches about the value of cooperation. "Swimmy" solves the problem of being a very small fish by banding together with other small fish as a way of protecting themselves from much larger fish. The illustrations by the author depict the underwater world in beautiful soft colors. 3*

Payne, Lauren Murphy

Illustrated by Claudia Rohling

We Can Get Along: A Child's Book of Choices

Minneapolis, MN: Free Spirit Publishing, Inc. (1997)

This book provides children with language for how to get along with their peers. The little stories acknowledge that sometimes conflicts arise but, with practice on "using our words," they usually can be resolved peacefully.

Pellegrini, Nina

Illustrated by Nina Pelligrini

Families Are Different

New York: Holiday House (1991)

A family story about trans-racial adoption is told in a simple, matter-of-fact way that young children can understand. It addresses the mixed emotions that arise when a child looks different from her or his parents, and compares many types of families bound together by love. 3*

Prelutsky, Jack
Illustrated by Dyanna Wolcott
Dog Days: Rhymes Around the Year
New York: Knopf (1999)
Four-line poems are a wonderful introduction to simple rhymes. Each poem features a dog celebrating what is special about each month of the year. Learning about the way words can rhyme from a preeminent children's poet will help children develop poems of their own. 3*

Rogers, Fred
Making Friends
New York: A PaperStar Book: Penguin Putnam Books for Young Readers (1996)
Illustrated with photographs of diverse children at play in preschool settings, Mr. Rogers helps young children explore the many aspects of friendship—playing, sharing ideas and secrets, sharing, not sharing. With simple language, the positive and negative feelings associated with friendship are discussed. 3*

Wells, Rosemary
Yoko
New York: Hyperion Books for Children (1998)
Using animal figures to represent a preschool class, Yoko addresses issues of hurtful teasing and inadequate adult intervention. When Yoko brings her favorite sushi lunch to school in a willow covered cooler, she is teased and insulted by other children who are unfamiliar with this type of food. Attempts by the teacher to first not take the insult seriously, and then create an "International Foods Day," don't work. Finally, one brave (and hungry) child tastes the sushi. The story helps children understand that sometimes trying the unfamiliar can result making new friends and learning to like new things. 3*

Van Genechten, Guido
Flop-Ear
Hauppauge, NY: Barron's Educational Services (2001)
The story of Flop-Ear addresses difference in a humorous and charming way. Flop-Ear is a rabbit who is taunted and teased because one of his ears does not stand up like the other, and like most rabbit ears. Flop-Ear devises many funny ways to make his ear stand up with no success. After being assured by a doctor that his ear is fine, Flop-Ear gains confidence in the way his ears are made. 3*

Zolotow, Charlotte
Pictures by William Pène Du Bois
William's Doll
New York: Harper Trophy Edition (1985)
This classic story addresses gender stereotyping in an engrossing way that has engaged young children since it was first published in 1972. William's brother and his brother's friend taunt and tease William because he wants a doll. William's father ignores his request for a doll, and brings him typical "boy" toys instead. William's grandmother understands his desire to have a doll, and explains the reason to William's father (her son). William wants a doll so he can practice being a father, just as girls practice being mothers through doll play.

Books for Adults Who Work With Children

Beane, Allan L.
The Bully Free Classroom
Minneapolis, MN: Free Spirit Publishing, Inc. (1999)
Although the activities are geared for grades K-8, this book contains many useful resources and ideas that can be modified for preschool. The bibliography of children's books lists several titles suitable for children of all ages.

Freedman, Judith S.
Easing the Teasing
Chicago: Contemporary Books (2002)
This guide, written for parents, can also be helpful to teachers who want to understand why some children tease and why others are targets for teasing. The strategies for children are most appropriate for elementary age students, but they spark some ideas for use with preschoolers.

Katch, Jane
They Don't Like Me: Lessons on Bullying and Teasing From a Preschool Classroom
Boston: Beacon Press (2003)
This is a first-hand account of how a preschool teacher addresses teasing, bullying, and exclusion in a preschool class. Especially helpful is how she handles one child who is a constant source of troublesome behavior that disrupts the usual smooth flow of the daily classroom life.

Levin, Diane E.
Teaching Young Children in Violent Times: Building a Peaecable Classroom
Cambridge, MA: Educators for Social Responsibility (1994)
This book is an excellent source of practical ideas for creating a peaceful, safe environment for preschoolers. Especially useful are the classroom management and planning tools for teachers, e.g., job charts, graphs that help children organize their thoughts and feelings, and instructions for creating curriculum webs to help teachers plan for individual children and keep tabs on progress.

Olweus, Dan
Bullying in Schools: What We Know and What We Can Do
Cambridge, MA: Blackwell Publishers, Inc. (1993)
Olweus is the leading authority nationally and internationally on the topic of teasing and bullying. This book describes Olweus' years of research on teasing and bullying in his native Norway and his renowned school-wide model.

Paley, Vivian Gussin
The Kindness of Children
Boston: Harvard University Press (1999)
Vivian Gussin Paley's deep respect for children shines throughout this book. Her insights help her to find incidents of children's kindness to each other that might not be noticed. She shares her stories with other children, thereby inspiring them to be kind. And, she uses these stories as teaching tools for her work with teachers.

Paley, Vivian Gussin
You Can't Say You Can't Play
Boston: Harvard University Press (1992)
A classic Paley book that has inspired teachers everywhere to change how they work with children. Paley tries the phrase, "You can't say you can't play," with her own kindergarten class in an attempt to reduce the teasing and exclusion that are so hurtful to the children who are always left out. She vividly describes the struggle with the concept that ensues during the school year. The rewards in terms of inclusion and the freeing up of children's play, especially regarding gender roles, makes for a much stronger learning environment by year's end.

Teaching Tolerance Project of the Southern Poverty Law Center
Starting Small: Teaching Tolerance in Preschool and the Early Grades
Starting Small video also available. [Note: This book and video set are available free of charge to schools].
Montgomery, AL: Southern Poverty Law Center (1997)
This book is full of practical suggestions about how to create a preschool community of children that gain ideas about cooperation and citizenship from the beginning of their school experience. The video, featuring Vivian Gussin Paley as the narrator, shows several preschool programs that are carrying out the themes of respect for diversity, peaceful problem solving, building community, and developing citizenship.

Websites

www.freespirit.org

This website lists all of Freespirit's publications and offers ideas for projects that children and parents can do together. The Ask Our Authors section invites teachers, parents, and children to ask questions that are answered by writers whose works are published by Freespirit.

www.ghbooks.com

Gryphon House publishes and distributes high-quality resources for teachers and parents. The website has a newsletter, and an online catalog of early childhood resource books for teachers and parents.

www.naeyc.org

The website of the National Association for the Education of Young Children is a valuable resource for all aspects of early childhood education. You will find position statements on The Code of Ethical Conduct, Media Violence in Children's Lives, and Violence in the Lives of Children. The site also offers information of professional development, policy, and myriad issues pertinent to quality early childhood education.

www.teachingtolerance.org

This website comes out of the Southern Poverty Law Center, an organization that has developed programs and materials around issues of tolerance for many years. The website offers Mix It Up Activity Booklets for grades K-6, online activities for parents and suggestions for things to talk about with kids. You can click on teachers, parents, or kids and find very practical ideas.

www.ZinktheZebra.org

The website is from a foundation that addresses differences and ideas about getting along. "How to Cope With Bullies" is a web page with useful tips for parents (or teachers) about talking about teasing and bullying with children.

Index

Preschool Classroom Management

150 Teacher-Tested Techniques
Laverne Warner and Sharon Ann Lynch

An essential resource that all teachers will appreciate! Written by two experienced teachers, *Preschool Classroom Management* offers solutions and suggestions to help you address behavior issues in the classroom. Chapters include working with challenging behaviors, building a caring community in the classroom, teacher tips and techniques, and dealing with daily routines and schedules. 224 pages. 2004.

Gryphon House | 15524

The Values Book

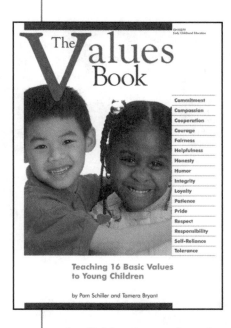

Teaching 16 Basic Values to Young Children
Pam Schiller and Tamera Bryant

Young children learn best by doing, and that includes learning values. *The Values Book* addresses 16 different values and is packed with easy activities, projects, and ideas to help children learn values and build character. The perfect book to introduce and strengthen the teaching of values in any early childhood classroom or home. 168 pages. 1998.

Gryphon House | 15279

◆ *Early Childhood News* **Directors' Choice Award**
◆ **Benjamin Franklin Award**

Available at your favorite bookstore, school supply store, or order from Gryphon House at 800.638.0928 or www.ghbooks.com.

The Peaceful Classroom

162 Easy Activities to Teach Preschoolers Compassion and Cooperation

Charles A. Smith, Ph.D

Through these engaging group activities, children learn to make friends, cooperate with others, and respect each other's feelings and differences. Activities foster sharing and caring through music, movement, puppet-making, playdough fun, gardening, and more. 208 pages. 1993.

Gryphon House | 15186

◆ **Benjamin Franklin Award**

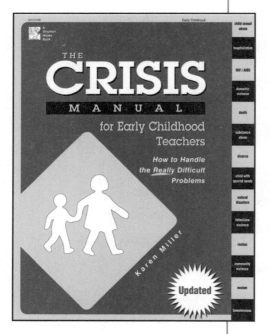

The Crisis Manual for Early Childhood Teachers, Updated

How to Handle the Really Difficult Problems

Karen Miller

The essential book to help you face those really difficult issues in the classroom. Learn practical strategies that address the most challenging problems you may encounter as a teacher, such as a death of a family member, domestic violence, substance abuse, sexual abuse, homelessness, natural disasters, and children with HIV/AIDS.
384 pages. 2003.

Gryphon House | 13748

◆ **Benjamin Franklin Award**